Friday Night Lights
for Fathers and Daughters

10 Life Lessons.
10 Faith-Driven Episodes.
Lifetime Memories.

MARK LAMASTER

ᚷAUTHOR ACADEMY elite

5-4-2018

Also by Mark LaMaster
Friday Night Lights for Fathers and Sons

ISBN: 978-1-64085-146-7
Library of Congress Control Number: 2018937438

I first met Mark LaMaster when he accepted my invitation to feature him in *DADLY Dads: Parents of the 21st Century*, the first coffee table book to showcase the value of fathers as parents. *Friday Night Lights for Fathers and Daughters* does a great job to highlight how important and valuable it is for a dad to develop a deeper and more meaningful relationship with his daughter during the teenage years. Not only will a dad get to know his daughter better, but more importantly, she will get to know and value a dad's role as a parent better!

Hogan Hilling
Founder, United We Parent
Creator of the DADLY Book Series
Nationally recognized and OPRAH-approved
author of 12 parenting books
www.UnitedWeParent.com

I have three wonderful daughters who are now beautifully mature women. When they were young, I ached to transmit really important life information to them—but found it hard. Mark LaMaster's *Friday Night Lights for Fathers and Daughters* is a "tool" I wish had been available back then. The good news for you dads of daughters today is that you now have it—a tool that can help you not only communicate, BUT gives you an excuse and a way to discuss the really important themes and questions of life—faith, body image, friends, social media, passion and calling, gratitude, boys, and sex.

Need I say more? Please get this book and use it to help motivate and guide you to a deeper relationship with that daughter or those daughters you love so very much. You will be glad you did.

Joe S. McIlhaney, MD
Founder/Chairman, The Medical
Institute for Sexual Health
Coauthor of *Hooked* and *Girls Uncovered*

I first met Mark LaMaster through various FCA activities with his kids. Since then, Mark has proven that he has a passion for faith-focused parenting. Whether it is coaching youth flag football, speaking at a halftime huddle, or as the guest speaker at an awards ceremony, Mark inspires parents to spend intentional time with their kids.

The relationship between a father and his daughter is a very special relationship. In *Friday Night Lights for Fathers and Daughters*, Mark has created a fun and interactive way for dads to get to know their daughters better, for daughters to learn more about their dads, and for both to grow closer to God. I am looking forward to going through this with my daughter Claire as she gets older. Pick up your copy today, and begin the journey!

James Bolin
Fellowship of Christian Athletes (FCA)
Southeast Minnesota Area Director
My.FCA.org/jamesbolin

Friday Night Lights for Fathers and Daughters is a creative way for dads to connect with their daughters. Many dads begin to distance themselves from their daughters as they become young women. Mark makes it easy. Every activity is planned out for you—questions and all! Not only will you get to know your daughter better, but she will get to know you better as well.

Rick A. Morris, PMP, ITIL, CSAM
John Maxwell Certified Speaker, Mentor, Coach
Owner / President R² Consulting, LLC
Host of "The Work/Life Balance"
rsquaredconsulting.com

Just because I've been labeled the expert on "Men Raised by Women," it doesn't mean I have all the answers. When men ask me for help raising their daughters, there really is only one response (because I'm in the same boat)—Mark LaMaster is the expert you need! As a father of an adopted daughter, I don't know all the challenges, but it's still my life's purpose to be the dad she needs. We are all working on it, and we all need help. Mark's *Friday Night Lights for Fathers and Daughters* provides us dads with a guidebook to help lead our daughters to become the young women they were designed to be.

John P. Dennis
Author, ***Men Raised by Women: What He Won't Tell Mom***
The Single Mom's Coach
The Step-Dad's Confidant
The Male Mentorship Guru
JohnPDennis.com

I love how Mark uses his God-given creativity to design unique "Daddy-Daughter Dates" in *Friday Night Lights for Fathers and Daughters*! It's so encouraging to see fathers stepping up and fully embracing the call to lead and love their daughters well. If you're a dad who desires to deepen and strengthen your relationship with your priceless princess, grab this book!"

Livy Jarmusch
Founder of *Crown of Beauty* Magazine
Author of the teen devotional, *Secrets of Royalty*

Mark nails it with his second book, *Friday Night Lights for Fathers and Daughters*. If you, like many other dads, are struggling with your father/daughter relationship, Mark's book provides a roadmap that will help you connect like never before. This book will help you develop the relationship with your daughter that you always wanted.

Brandon Handley
Founder, Fatherhood for the Rest of Us
FatherhoodfortheRestofUs.com

I read Mark's first book, *Friday Night Lights for Fathers and Sons* and loved it. In fact, my only disappointment was that I have a daughter. Immediately, I asked Mark if he had plans for a book to address the father/daughter relationship. I am genuinely excited about this book.

As a pastor and discipleship coach, an insecurity that I find in men is that they don't know how to relate to their daughters. Our daughters need their father's *presence* more than anything else from him. As they become women, they get a sense of confidence and independence from having a father who is not afraid to listen nor intimidated by emotional differences. How our daughters think men view them comes from their relationship with their father and this resonates into their future relationships.

If you want your daughter to develop an identity rooted in Jesus rather than the affirmation and affection of romantic relationships, being a present father will give her a head start. Mark's book creates great environments to lead your daughter to a healthy father/daughter relationship as well as teaching her to get her sense of worth from Christ.

Scott Perkins
Pastor, Discipleship Coach, and Author
Tree of Lies: Transforming Decisions, Behaviors, and
Relationships By Gaining Perspective On Your Identity in Christ
PerkinsPerspectives.com

We don't read the instructions or ask for directions. Why? We're men. But then, we have a daughter, and we have no idea which instructions or directions to follow. Too many of us allow society, culture, and the schools to teach our daughters when all they wanted was Daddy.

LaMaster has created an interactive experience for us all to follow if you have a teenage daughter or soon will (like me). It will take effort, but that's the beauty. Our daughters are wired emotionally, and they want our time and effort. This book will absolutely connect you and your princess to God and to each other in a new and exciting way. And as I always say in my work with dads, "Creativity leads to connection, and connection leads to conversation." LaMaster truly understands this and will help you if you give this book your effort."

Ken Carfagno
Founder, Dadnamics

For Nar.
God truly blessed me when he gave me you.
I love you thiiiiiiiis much!

CONTENTS

ACT II—THE SEASON

FOREWORD

I fell to my knees in the middle of my government-issued apartment and cried loud tears of agony and defeat as I pressed my exhausted body onto the cold bathroom floor. I couldn't go on. A young single mother of two small children, it seemed the weight of the world had finally won, and all I could think was that there was no way out. I had no money, no friends, and no hope. I cried out to the God of my childhood—certain he didn't exist—or if he did, he surely couldn't hear me. My little toddling boy came into the bathroom that night and patted his weary mother on the back and said, "It's otay, Momma. It's otay." With tears streaming down my face, I looked into the eyes of my son, certain I was a complete failure as a mother. I realized that everything I had endured in my own childhood, I was now duplicating in my children's childhood.

My mother was killed when I was only a year old. I was raised by my father who used alcohol and women to cope with the devastation of my mother's death. My dad was a provider. He was born in 1935 in rural Mississippi and the hard work of his childhood parlayed into an unparalleled work ethic that he then instilled into me. For that, I am thankful. He was a deacon at the local Baptist church before my mother was killed, and church attendance and a life for Christ were principles he instilled in me early on. Likewise, I am thankful. But the years of alcohol abuse and the undealt pain of his past caught up to him. He worked many hours away from home, married six times, and drank himself into a stupor many nights—leaving me desperate for attention in all the wrong places.

Is it any wonder I had two children outside of marriage by the time I was 19? Or that I chased a dead-end, abusive, relationship for seven years before I had the strength to move on? That's why Mark LaMaster's *Friday Night Lights for Fathers and Daughters* is so important. The need for fathers and daughters to engage in meaningful conversation and develop life-long, life-giving relationships is perhaps the most important a daughter can ever know. It lays the groundwork for her future.

My own experiences culminated into an eventual passion to empower single mothers to raise their children in Christian homes. Now married, I saw my husband's love for my children (whom he adopted) and eventually for our own child, and I saw how impactful it was when done right. I saw how the love he has for our daughters have molded them to be confident, beautiful, strong, women of God, who know who they are and more importantly, *whose* they are. I saw how my father's inadequacies led me down a path that created destruction and pain. Even still, I became more intimately aware of my Heavenly Father's love through it all. No matter where you fall on your fathering path, this book can help you be a better dad.

Today, I have the great privilege of working with more than 50,000 single mothers each year through The Life of a Single Mom Ministries. We have worked with more than 1,500 churches, countless prison systems, community groups, and government organizations to empower every single mother to rise up and raise her children in the way they should go. And the work has been powerful. The hand of God has been so evident in the journey. But I can't help but to think how much more beautiful it would be if I worked myself right out of a job!

What if every father parented his child with love, compassion, and intention? What if all fathers were active missionaries on a mission to see their children serve the Lord? So, thank you for picking up this book. Thank you for having a heart to be the dad God has called you to be, for you will surely never know the eternal impact you are making on those precious ones you call "daughter."

—Jennifer Maggio, Chief Executive Officer/Founder

The Life of a Single Mom Ministries

Certain is it that there is no kind of affection so purely angelic as of a father to a daughter. In love to our wives there is desire; to our sons, ambition; but to our daughters there is something which there are no words to express.

—*Joseph Addison*

YOUR FREE GIFT

As a way of saying thank you for buying my book, I'm offering a **FREE** *Friday Night Lights for Fathers and Daughters Guide* that's exclusive to readers of *Friday Night Lights for Fathers and Daughters*.

The *Friday Night Lights for Fathers and Daughters Guide* includes everything you need to get started on your 10-Episode season with your daughter—a printable overview of each of the 10 Episodes, extra Episode ideas, and an inspirational video from me.

You can pick up everything you need to get started on your 10-Episode season with your daughter with your *Friday Night Lights for Fathers and Daughters Guide* by clicking here:

MarkLaMaster.com/daughterguide

HYPERLINKS INCLUDED

The ebook version of *Friday Night Lights for Fathers and Daughters* includes over 50 hyperlinks to resources and printables that will enhance your experience throughout your 10-Episode season. I wanted to list them all out here, but my editor suggested that it would have been an unpleasant reading experience (and also potentially frustrating because some of the websites will most likely change in the future).

Therefore, I compiled all of the hyperlinks listed in this book at my website: MarkLaMaster.com/daughterlinks

Please note that some of the hyperlinks are affiliate links in which I will receive a small commission for each sale (at no extra cost to you).

JOIN THE FRIDAY NIGHT LIGHTS FOR FATHERS COMMUNITY

One final thing before you get started—I would like to officially invite you to become part of the Friday Night Lights for Fathers Community by joining the Friday Night Lights for Fathers Private Facebook Group.

Imagine a group of like-minded dads who want to develop deeper relationships with their kids. Inside the Friday Night Lights for Fathers Facebook Group, you will be able to:

- Share your *Friday Night Lights for Fathers and Daughters* and *Friday Night Lights for Fathers and Sons* experiences with other dads, such as:

    - Pictures

    - Video Clips

    - Comments

- Ask questions and help answer questions from other dads

- Give and seek encouragement

- Connect with dads from across the country

- Become part of a positive and encouraging community of dads!

JOIN TODAY

 xxv

AUTHOR'S NOTE

As Hannah, my daughter, has now entered her teenage years, I wanted to get a glimpse inside of her world while at the same time introducing her to mine. I wanted to better understand how Hannah viewed the world through her teenage mind. But, I also wanted to teach her what guys think about and how we view the world.

Not only did I want to get to know my daughter better, but I wanted to find new ways to help lead both of us closer to God.

Ever since the release of my book, *Friday Night Lights for Fathers and Sons*, parents have been asking me questions like, "When is the book for daughters coming out?" or "Do you plan to write something similar for girls?"

Well, I have to be honest, it has always been part of the plan, but I wanted to be absolutely sure that I had some real-life experience being a dad to a teenage daughter. And, man oh man, did I learn a lesson—be careful what you ask for! Through my daughter's experiences, I was able to better understand how the teenage girl's mind works, the situations she endures, and how they carve out their pecking order as they transition from a girl to a young woman. It was almost as if God held me back in my writing so I could better convey the parenting lessons I had learned.

This book is a culmination of my experiences with my daughter, my wife, my clients, and my research from some very dedicated individuals.

This book is for you if you are raising a tween or teenage daughter and need some encouragement and reassurance that you are on the right path. This book is also for you if you feel a bit discouraged or even defeated as a dad. Along the way, though, I will challenge you, the statistics will shock you, and the stories will surprise you.

Dads, we have an awesome responsibility in raising our daughters to become the young women they were created and designed to be. Whether you are a dad, adoptive dad, foster dad, step-dad, divorced dad, single dad, grandpa, uncle, or any other man raising a tween to teenage daughter, I wrote this book to help you navigate through these transformative years in a young woman's life.

Mark LaMaster

ACT I:
PRE-PRODUCTION

INTRODUCTION

I remember the nanosecond my daughter, Hannah, was born. I should have known immediately how Hannah would impact my life, but I honestly did not know what journey I had just embarked upon.

Hannah was our first child. Jen and I—call us old-fashioned—had decided to sidestep the ultrasound's ability to distinguish gender and wait for the ultimate surprise of pink or blue on our new child's birthday.

Yes, we had our children before the "gender reveal party" trend. No Team Pink or Team Blue invites were sent out. In fact, Hannah was born pre-iPhone and pre-Facebook.

Despite having a medical background, I innocently assumed Jen's labor would be textbook and without complications.

I was wrong. Several hours into labor, the labor and delivery nurse noticed some concerning traces on the monitor. I had been sitting next to Jen, holding her hand, and coaching her through her breathing exercises as we had practiced during our childbirth classes the weeks prior. The next thing I knew, a team of caregivers entered the room and surrounded Jen. I was asked to move away from the bed and ended up sitting on the windowsill of the hospital room.

Accustomed to being at the bedside, I now found myself miles away from my wife and unborn child, unable to help, let alone hold my bride's hand.

I understood the situation but still wanted back in the circle of action. As they started a new intravenous line, hung new medications, repositioned my wife, and closely watched both my wife's and unborn baby's vital signs, all I could do was pray. And pray I did!

My naïve visions of a "normal" labor suddenly switched to a check-in with my Creator. It was almost as if God were reminding me that I needed Him now more than ever. It was as if He were guiding me to look up rather than looking at the monitors—allowing the experts to care for my wife and child-to-be.

I can vividly remember my dad daydreams, looking forward to the mystery of fatherhood I had envisioned for so long. During that time on the windowsill, God sent a sense of calmness to me that I had never experienced before. It was surreal, and I long to experience that calmness again.

Time seemed to stand still even though I could see the flurry of activity around Jen's hospital bed. Through it all, Jen's eyes sparkled with determination of giving birth to our new little miracle.

Before I knew it, Jen and the baby were stable once again, thanks to the keen awareness of the nurse and the quick response of the labor and delivery team.

But we were not out of the woods quite yet. All of the interventions to slow down Jen's contractions had caused a delay in delivery. So, we waited. I took my spot next to Jen's bed, held her hand, and we waited. The obstetrician informed us that it would still be a few hours before our new baby would be born. She also let us know she was headed across the street to grab some dinner, but assured us her colleague was right next door and would be available should we need him.

Only a few minutes after our obstetrician left, Jen's contractions increased in strength and intervals. The nurse peeked into our room, assessed Jen, and pulled the head obstetrician from the next room. We didn't know it at the time, but we would be brand new parents within 15 minutes.

The team acted in concert with each other, rattling off medical terms, handing off equipment, and working with the efficiency of a professional sports team.

Jen was now in a lot of pain, squeezing my hand so hard it should probably have fallen off. I was focused on Jen, but was also excited to meet my new baby. At one point, the nurse said, your baby has a head of red hair. There it was, the first physical description I would ever have of my baby—red hair. I could barely take the suspense any longer. Jen could barely take the pain any longer.

Then it happened, but not how I imagined it would happen. The nurse said, "Congratulations, you now have a brand-new baby fajklf;ajf!" She and the rest of the medical team were smiling from ear to ear as if it was the first time they had helped birth a new child.

Jen was looking at me, and I was looking at her for the answer. Neither of us understood what the nurse had said, and I had to ask her to repeat it. She said, more clearly this time, "It's a GIRL!"

For whatever reason, our new bundle of joy must have been a bit frustrated at the obstetrician and decided to poop all over the head obstetrician. I could tell by the look on his face that this hadn't happened to him in some time. I also caught the nurses in the room smirking at each other as if this were an inside joke amongst the team.

After our brand-new baby girl was cleaned off, the nurse presented her to Jen and laid this little miracle on Jen's chest. In a few minutes, after touching my baby girl's head for the first time, I leaned over and gave her the first kiss from her daddy.

Soon, I would be cutting her umbilical cord, helping to cover her perfectly round head with a tiny cap and cuddling her up in the infamous blanket wrap. Moments later, I went to the waiting room to tell my family that Jen and I were now the proud parents of a little girl, Hannah Rae!

As I write this, I have chills on the back of my neck and goosebumps on my arms.

My visions of witnessing my daughter's birth were a far cry from the "sugar and spice and everything nice" vision, as were the many experiences I have encountered in raising her as a tween and teen. But I can proudly say that despite the ups and downs of parenting during this somewhat tumultuous stage, I have continually developed a deeper and more meaningful relationship with my daughter. I wrote this book for those of you who would also like to develop the same kind of relationship with your own daughter(s).

The book is divided into three main parts which I have aptly named "Acts." For those of you that have read and gone through my first book, *Friday Night Lights for Fathers and Sons*, you will notice a similar format. However, instead of scheduling a 10-Game Day season with your daughter, you will be producing your very own 10-Episode reality TV series season with her.

Why Episodes rather than Game Days?

I chose Episodes for several practical and strategic reasons. First of all, it's popular. Binge-watching TV series has become the new pastime of America. According to Deloitte's 11th Digital Democracy Survey, 73 percent of us binge watch TV. Nearly 90% of your kids binge watch weekly.[1] Netflix alone has over 100 million subscribers.[2]

Secondly, well-done TV series leave you wanting more each week. In the old-fashioned format of network TV series, we had to wait a whole week to learn about all of the open-ended plot twists from the week before. Whether or not a TV series is traditional or streamed, the best ones create anticipation and excitement for the future. I wanted my daughter to look forward to spending time with me during each Episode. I also wanted her to anticipate the next

Episode and be excited about the Red Carpet Interviews. I want this for you and your daughters as well.

The third reason I went with the Episode theme is this little four letter word—T-I-M-E. If most of us filled out a time journal, we would likely discover that we spend more time watching our favorite TV series than we do with our daughters. Consider the recent stats from Netflix—Americans, on average, finish an entire season of a show in one week, watching about two hours a day and up to five, even six episodes in one setting.[3]

The fourth and final reason I chose the Episode theme is because it is FUN! Throughout your 10-Episode Season, you and your daughter will develop a deeper and more meaningful relationship with each other and with God and will have a blast doing it!

Here is the breakdown of the book:

Act I: Pre-Production

A Dad's Particular Set of Skills

During Act I, we will squash out many myths about fatherhood which have become commonplace in our broken world by discussing *A Dad's Particular Set of Skills*. Stories will be shared and research will be revealed as to why you matter to your daughter, especially during the critical phase of adolescence as her brain and body go through some of the most dramatic transformations she will ever experience.

Act II: The 10-Episode Season

To help provide both you and your daughter with consistency and familiarity, each Episode will follow the same basic format:

I. 🎬 Pilot or Episode Title

To maintain the theme of the TV and movie industry, each Episode title will give some hint about the Episode's theme.

II. 🎞 Episode Guide

The Episode Guide serves as a quick glance overview of the theme, Bible verse, Episode location, and activity.

a. *Theme*

The theme is the overall life lesson for the entire Episode.

b. *"SCRIPT"-ure*

Each TV series needs the best scriptwriters available—this book happens to have the best: God. Each life lesson is based on scripture.

c. *Set Location*

A quick check on the Set Location will help you know where each Episode will be filmed. More details will be provided in The Live Shoot!

d. *3-2-1 Action! Activity*

A brief glimpse of each Episode's interactive activity may be found here.

III. 📢 The Pitch

Before any TV series makes it to prime time, the writers must make the pitch to the producers. The Pitch will provide you, Dad, with the background, topic research and statistics, and real-life stories that will help you pass on the life lesson of each Episode.

IV. 🎬 Behind the Scenes Setup (for Dad)

This section provides a step-by-step plan for you to successfully plan out each Episode and includes the following:

> a. *Set Location*
> A detailed description of each location for you to scout out for each Live Shoot!
>
> b. *3-2-1 Action! Activity Overview*
> This overview begins to set the stage for The Live Shoot!
>
> c. *Stage Checklist*
> I have done my best to list out everything that you will need for each Episode in the Stage Checklist.

V. 📹 The Live Shoot!

Beginning with the customizable Pre-Episode Prayer, The Live Shoot! will walk you through each Episode's 3-2-1 Action Activity step-by-step and question by question.

VI. 🎟 Backstage Pass

The Backstage Pass is, I believe, the most important part of each Episode. This is where you and your daughter will ask each other the tough and awkward questions that will help you bond like never before as father and daughter.

VII. 🎤 Red Carpet Interview

Deep down, I think each of us has wanted to walk within the ropes of the red carpet at one time in our lives. The Red Carpet Interview gives both you and your daughter the opportunity to do so.

For the Red Carpet Interview, you will need a camera. You will begin by having your daughter record you as she asks you the Red Carpet Interview Questions for Dad. You will follow by filming your daughter as you ask her the Red Carpet Interview Questions for Daughter.

The video that you capture is priceless. Take it from a guy who rarely takes pictures or videos of my kids' activities. The video footage provides a slice of time in both you and your daughter's lives that you will cherish for as long as you live.

I would be honored if you would be willing to share any video clips from your Episodes with me as well as other dads going through their own 10-Episode *Friday Night Lights for Fathers and Daughters* Season. If you are willing to share, please join the *Friday Night Lights for Fathers Private Facebook Group*-where all of us dads can share, encourage, and inspire other dads to develop deeper and more meaningful relationships with our kids.

VIII. 🎬 Hannah's Take

My daughter, Hannah, has been an outstanding consultant to me during my writing and creative process. I asked Hannah to write down her thoughts and feedback about each Episode in this section. I wanted your daughter to have first-hand insight through a peer's viewpoint for each Episode. Hannah hopes your daughter finds value in it.

ACT III: The Ceremony

🏆 The Dad'n'Me Award Ceremony

Staying in line with the TV series theme, I thought it only natural to help you plan a celebrity-style award show. The Dad'n'Me Award Ceremony is simply that—a ceremony to seal the 10-Episode season you and your daughter have created together.

Your Award Ceremony may be as formal or as informal as you wish. The guest list may include immediate family only or as many influencers in your daughter's life as you choose.

A sample script is provided, and I have even created matching awards for both you and your daughter ("connection keychains").

Prayer to Accept Jesus Christ
Undoubtedly, the most impactful and life-changing words of this entire book. If you, your daughter, or someone you know would like to accept Jesus Christ into their life, I have added this simple, but powerful prayer.

A couple of final notes and tips as you progress throughout your 10-Episode season:

- Make sure to grab all of the bonus resources I have for you and your daughter throughout the book. They are FREE. Just look for the stage lighting symbol like the one below:

- Compile all of your videos and make sure to back each Episode up on your computer, a cloud drive, or an external hard drive.

- Remember, this is not a season of perfection, but of connection. Each Episode will not always go as planned—believe me, I know first-hand.

- Lastly, when in doubt, always remember Proverbs 3:5, "Trust in the LORD with all your heart and lean not on your own understanding."

I have tried my absolute best to make this book as user-friendly and as comprehensive as possible for you. If you have any questions, need some clarity, or just want to say hi, do not hesitate to shoot me an email at Mark@MarkLaMaster.com or check out what else I am up to at MarkLaMaster.com

A DAD'S PARTICULAR SET OF SKILLS

Despite what you have been led to believe, your role as a dad is essential in raising your daughter. Not only is it evident in the Bible, but science is now proving it.

I could go on and on about how today's culture has emasculated dads to the point of defeat, how most television shows portray dads as the blubbering idiot (think Homer Simpson), how most commercials picture dads as inept (think the Huggies "Dad Test" commercial), or how divorce courts still prefer a mother's custody over a father's, but I think most of us are past all of this and are moving on.

One of the biggest reasons I believe we are moving on is because dads like you and me are standing up for what we already know is true—we matter!

Whether you are a dad, stepdad, adoptive dad, single dad, divorced dad, or any male father figure, you have been gifted with unique skills only you can provide for your daughter.

As I am writing this, I can't help but think of one of my favorite dad quotes ever:

> "..., but what I do have is a very particular set of skills.
> Skills I have acquired over a very long career ..."
> —Liam Neeson in the movie, *Taken*[1]

If you have seen *Taken*, you have likely tried your hand at impersonating this infamous phone speech. No one does it as well as Liam Neeson, sorry.

The truth is, you do have a 'very particular set of skills' that God created just for dads.

Yes, the science has been slow to seep into the mainstream media, but more and more content is beginning to create a stir. *USA Today* even ran an article on the science of fatherhood titled, "Why Dads Matter, According to Science." The author, sounding almost surprised, starts his article with the following statement: "An involved father's impact is more than a few good stories, notable quips and hard-learned lessons. Science proves he's worth more."[2]

In this 2017 article, Dr. Kyle Pruett, a child psychiatrist and clinical professor at the Yale School of Medicine, cites examples from study after study touting the scientific benefits for kids with involved fathers. Here are a few of the highlights:

- They're less likely to gender stereotype
- They stay at their job longer
- They do better in school
- They're more likely to delay sex
- They're less likely to be criminals[2]

If you look at the *USA Today* article as what it truly is, then you will understand that the bullet points only represent small snippets of the research that is actually being done.

As I began looking into what science has to say about fatherhood, I ran across Paul Raeburn's work. Paul is a journalist who became curious about whether or not he, as a dad, mattered. With a journalist's lens, he set out to find out the answer to the question: Can science prove whether or not fathers matter?

I picked up a copy of his book, *Do Fathers Matter? What Science is Telling Us About the Parent We've Overlooked,* and couldn't put it down.

Paul writes, "Until recently, when we thought about the roles of fathers in the family, we relied on hunches, instincts, prejudice, and misinformation, rather than real understanding." He goes on to expose that as recently as 2006; parenting research was predominantly mother-focused as compared to fathers—with only 11% of the research being father-focused.[3]

However, Raeburn points out that even though father-focused research still lags behind, "psychologists, biologists, sociologists, and neuroscientists have begun to generate solid scientific data on why fathers behave the way they do—and why it matters to children."[3]

As I read through study after study and story after story, I couldn't help but wonder why I had never heard this information. One particular study caught my attention—mostly because it had to do with the relationship between a father and his daughter. I knew immediately that I wanted to share it with you in this book. Here is a summary of the study.

In 2011, Frayser High School in Memphis, Tennessee, made headlines when it was revealed that nearly 20% of their female students were pregnant or had recently given birth. Yes, 90 high schoolers in the same school pregnant at the same time.

The school's administration, based on expert counsel, was quick to blame MTV's *Teen Mom* and *16 and Pregnant* shows. While this may very well have had some part to do with this sudden spike in teen pregnancies, two curious psychologists had a different perspective.

Sarah E. Hill and Danielle J. DelPriore, psychologists at Texas Christian University, found another reason. They noticed that nearly one in four households in Tennessee was headed by a single mother. They were on to something, "For several decades and across numerous samples, researchers have revealed a robust association between father absence—both physical and psychological—and accelerated reproductive development and sexual risk taking in daughters."[3]

Why was this happening? Hill believes "When dad is absent, it basically provides young girls with a cue about what the future holds for them in terms of the mating system . . . she gets the message that men don't stick around long . . . so finding a man requires quick action and the sooner she is ready to have children, the better."[3]

The opposite is true as well. If the girl is raised in a home where both mom and dad are present, she feels more secure, has more time to start having kids, and can prepare for motherhood over time.

Rather than blaming MTV, Hill and DelPriore used old-fashioned research to discover how fathers impact the lives of their daughters.

This information led Hill and DelPriore to devise a study to determine whether or not a disengaged or absent father influenced his daughter's attitude toward sexual behavior. The results may surprise you. As the researchers predicted, daughters of disengaged or absent fathers were more "sexually unrestrictive." Hill then shares that girls with disengaged dads, "reported having more favorable attitudes toward short-term sexual encounters; they didn't see love as necessary for sex to occur."[3]

Dads, scientific study after scientific study are proving that we matter in the lives of our daughters. In this case, our presence and engagement help our daughters to understand that sex is more than just a short-term sexual encounter.

This is just one of many areas we positively influence the lives our children, and daughters specifically. Several organizations continue to track fatherhood research, notably, The National Fatherhood Initiative and The National Center for Fathering.

Instead of listing out all of the statistics, data, and studies on why you matter to your daughter, I am going to share nine of Dr. James Dobson's "11 Reasons Why Dads Matter to Their Daughters," from his book, *Dads and Daughters*:

1. Girls whose fathers provide warmth and control achieve **greater academic success.**

2. Girls who are close to their fathers exhibit **less anxiety** and withdrawal behaviors.

3. Parental connectedness is the *number one factor* in **preventing girls from engaging in premarital sex and indulging in drugs and alcohol.**

4. Daughters who believe that their fathers care about them have significantly fewer suicide attempts and **fewer instances of body dissatisfaction, depression, low self- esteem, substance abuse, and unhealthy weight.**

5. Girls with involved fathers are twice as likely to **stay in school.**

6. Girls with fathers or father figures **feel more protected**, are more likely to attempt college, and are less likely to drop out of college.

7. Girls with good fathers are **less likely to seek male attention by flaunting themselves.**

8. Girls who live with their mothers and fathers (as opposed to mothers only) have significantly **fewer growth and developmental delays, and fewer learning disorders, emotional disabilities, and behavioral problems.**

9. Girls do **better academically if their fathers establish rules and exhibit affection.**[4]

Dads, take it from Dr. Dobson, your relationship with your daughter will have life-long implications. You must choose whether or not they are life-giving or life-debilitating. This book was written for the former.

ACT II:
THE 10-EPISODE SEASON

Pilot Episode

Believe

🎞 Episode Guide

Theme
Faith

"SCRIPT"-ure

> *Now faith is the assurance of things hoped for, the conviction of things not seen. And without faith it is impossible to please him, for whoever would draw near to God must believe that he exists and that he rewards those who seek him.*
>
> *Hebrews 11:1,6*

Set Location
The perfect sunrise viewing spot

3-2-1 Action! Activity
Sunrise breakfast and "My One Word"

📣 The Pitch

It was a typical Sunday morning for this four-member family. Everyone was up by 7:00 am and was enjoying their morning routine, all assuming they would attend the 9:00 am church service. As the clock neared the normal departure time, the dad called a family pow-wow to discuss options for church this morning. Having just been told by his wife that it was baptism Sunday, this dad suddenly had a change of heart—baptisms made him feel awkward, guilty, and generally uncomfortable.

As the family gathered in the living room for their

pow-wow, the dad listed out the following options for church, with full disclosure that it was baptism Sunday:

1. Read two chapters of the Bible, do devotions, and watch a sermon online.

2. Do a family devotion and listen to the morning's sermon that would be posted online later that evening.

3. Go to church as planned.

The dad, in a most democratic way, said, "On the count of three, raise your hand and vote for the option you would like to do this morning." Secretly, the dad assumed his family would choose either option 1 or option 2. It had been a busy week—hosting Thanksgiving the weekend before and the Christmas season just about to kick into high gear. A day with no plans and no place to go would be a great way to recharge and get ready for the countdown to Christmas. Right?

Unfortunately, for the dad, and before he could even finish the rules of the voting process, his daughter spoke out, "No dad, we're going to church today." It wasn't rude, it wasn't snotty, and it certainly wasn't what the dad had expected. It was convicting!

The family finished their final last-minute morning rituals, piled into the car, and headed to church.

The dad didn't want to go, but "manned up," mostly because his daughter was so emphatic on going. *Why was she so set on going?* ran through his mind on their way to church.

The dad had been baptized as an infant and raised in the Lutheran church. His views on baptism were conflicting and confusing. Over the past decade or so, the baptisms he had witnessed were more of a production than he cared for, with professional video testimonies that almost seemed scripted. The dad had purposely avoided the last several baptism Sundays for his own selfish reasons.

As the family walked into the church that morning, the dad felt a sense of resistance he had never felt before. Of course, the first thing he saw was the rented, portable hot tub that would be the focus of today's service. He let his wife lead them to their seats, a row that was about as far from the hot tub as possible, perhaps unconsciously knowing her husband's current feelings about baptism.

The worship songs seem to last forever, the dad thought. When the music was over, he said to himself, *Good, now we can get these baptisms over*. Unfortunately, the pastor went out of order from previous baptism Sunday agendas—he started giving his sermon! *Seriously?* The dad was getting more impatient and felt his emotions moving toward anger.

The pastor was in the middle of a series on Acts and began preaching about Philip and how an angel of God instructed him to travel to a distant town. There, he met an Ethiopian eunuch who was reading from the scrolls of Isaiah.

The dad admitted to himself that the sermon had captured his attention and was a story he wasn't sure he had ever heard before. He found himself listening more intently, digging into his study Bible. He was even reading the study notes at the bottom of the page, wanting to better understand the scripture featured in the pastor's sermon.

Philip offered to help the Ethiopian interpret the book of Isaiah, and continued to tell him about the gospel of Jesus, about being born again in and through Christ through baptism. The dad was on the edge of his seat now, the resistance he had experienced when he entered the church had now exited his soul and was being filled with a new sensation, one he couldn't quite identify—yet.

As the pastor continued unpacking the story of Philip, he read Acts 8:36–39:

And as they were going along the road they came to some water, and the eunuch said, "See, here is water! What prevents me from being baptized?" And he commanded the chariot to stop, and they both went down into the water, Philip and the eunuch, and he baptized him.

The dad didn't hear much else the pastor said for the next few minutes. The Ethiopian eunuch's question struck deep within the dad's soul. "See, here is water! What prevents *me* from being baptized?"

A few minutes passed, and the dad heard the pastor wrapping up his message. The pastor spoke directly to those in attendance. He pointed to the baptism tub and said, "Here is water! What prevents *you* from being baptized?" He went on to invite anyone that felt led to be baptized to come and be born again.

The dad stood up and began walking up the stairs to the room the pastor directed him to go. It was as if he was being led by a power not of his own. Upon entering the room, he was welcomed with open arms and high fives, and began a brief baptismal interview before entering the baptismal tank.

As the dad was answering the questions, he was aware that another person had answered the pastor's call and had just entered the interview room. The only glimpse he caught of this person was a blur of red hair and whispers. The young woman sat at another table out of his sight.

As the dad was answering the final question, it became clear to him who the young woman was. It was his daughter! His daughter had followed him.

Within a few minutes, the father and daughter entered the baptism tub. The dad gave his heartfelt testimony to the nearly 200 people in the church and was baptized, just as the Ethiopian eunuch had done nearly 2,000 years ago.

What an amazing feeling this dad had just experienced, but it paled in comparison to what was to happen next. It was completely unscripted, unplanned, and incomprehensible. This dad, who was scheming to stay home from church, but went because his daughter led him, was now in a baptism tub, listening to his daughter's testimony of faith in Jesus Christ. Moments later, the dad, newly baptized, baptized his own daughter.

This story is filled with so many lessons, stories, and emotions. Right now, you might be wondering if this is a story I made up to fit the plot of this Episode.

This is a true baptismal story. In fact, it is the personal story of my daughter and I. It is a story that I would never have dreamed of, never imagined, and certainly never planned. It is a story of trusting in God and having the courage to be led by the Holy Spirit. It is a story of faith, a faith that can only come from a loving and all-knowing God.

When I abruptly stood up in the middle of the church service that day, my wife later told me that she assumed I was going to the restroom to avoid listening to the testimonies during the baptisms. Hannah told me she knew exactly what I was doing. She shared with me her ongoing conviction to become baptized over the last several months. Hannah would later reveal that the reason she decided to be baptized was because I would be with her.

Since the nanosecond that my precious little miracle was born into this world, I have never been prouder of her than I was on the day that she was born again—born into God's kingdom as an obedient follower of His son, Jesus Christ.

Dads, we are our daughters' heroes. It has never been so evident to me as on the day that we shared the same baptismal water, sharing our testimonies, and proclaiming our faith to our heavenly Father.

James MacDonald, founder and senior pastor of Harvest Bible Chapel, defines faith as "Believing the Word of God and acting upon it, no matter how [you] feel, because God promises a good result."[1]

Hannah and I believe in the Word of God and, on that particular Sunday morning, we acted upon it, regardless of how we felt, because we had faith that God promises a good result.

Today's "SCRIPT"-ure comes from Hebrews 11. The Holy Spirit spoke to me through the Word of God.

Now faith is the assurance of things hoped for, the conviction of things not seen. And without faith it is impossible to please him, for whoever would draw near to God must believe that he exists and that he rewards those who seek him.

Hebrews 11:1, 6

Our baptismal story is certainly powerful, but as I mentioned earlier, it was completely unplanned—or was it?

Looking back, I have come to realize that God had His fingerprints on every single detail of our baptismal day. Our spiritual journeys bring His plan to light. My walk with God had seen its share of peaks and valleys (mostly valleys) in the form of anxiety and depression a few years back. My anxiety and depression paralyzed me to the point I believed I had a terminal illness with only a few years to live. Only through the strength of my wife's faith was I eventually led to give my depression over to God.

About eleven months before Hannah stepped into the baptismal water, Hannah had a life-changing, faith-forming experience at a winter church camp. She answered the youth pastor's altar call and accepted Jesus Christ as her Savior. Ever since that camp, Hannah has not missed a day of daily devotions and time in His Word. She is a young woman on fire for the Lord, and I am so proud of her.

My point to you is that God will use any circumstance, any person, any suffering, any situation, or any success to show you His unfailing love for you and to lead you to a faith that He is real and loves you unconditionally.

As fathers, God instructs us to teach His commandments to our children. He makes it clear, though, that only He, through the Holy Spirit, can lead our children to God.

But, how do we, as dads, help lead our children to God, to accept Jesus Christ as their Savior, and to help the Holy Spirit churn inside our daughters' hearts?

Well, one answer to this question is what this Episode is all about. Let's pull the curtain back and peek behind the scenes to prepare for today's Live Shoot!

Behind the Scenes Setup (for Dad)

Set Location

Today's Episode will require that you do a bit of location scouting. You will be looking for a spot to watch a sunrise with your daughter. Why? Because watching the sunrise is one of the best ways to help our daughters visualize our faith in God.

In Lamentations 3:22–24, God tells us:

> *The Lord's unfailing love and mercy still continue,*
> *Fresh as the morning, as sure as the sunrise.*
> *The Lord is all I have, and so in him I put my hope. (GNT)*

As I opened my eyes one morning, I was greeted with a thin slice of the most beautiful sunrise I had seen in years. With only two or three inches not covered by our mini-blinds, our room was filled with a palette of brilliant oranges and reds that I had never before laid eyes on.

Knowing that sunrises change quickly, I gently woke Jen up and shared God's masterpiece sunrise with her. She got out of bed and opened the blinds. As she did, we both just sat silently and gave thanks to our Creator.

I had known for some time that the setting for the "Believe" Episode would be a sunrise, but that day, God confirmed it. His sunrise inspired me to finalize this Episode by the end of the day.

3-2-1 Action! Activity Overview

The goal of today's Episode is to help lead your daughter along her faith walk. Therefore, you and your daughter will be choosing your "One Word" during your sunrise adventure.

Stage Checklist

- Location choice

- Schedule The Live Shoot! with your daughter and put in on your calendar.

- Confirm the sunrise time and make sure to arrive at least 20–30 minutes early

- My One Word website (MyOneWord.org) and/or *My One Word* book

- The *Friday Night Lights for Fathers and Daughters* One Word Certificate at MarkLaMaster.com/oneword

- Blanket or event chairs

- An insulated mug full of hot cocoa, coffee, or juice

- Muffins/snack

Are you feeling good about today's Episode? Next up—The Live Shoot! It's almost Show Time. As you prepare for the Believe Episode, I encourage you to pray that the Holy Spirit will work through you and your daughter during your time together.

🎥 The Live Shoot!

As you and your daughter are fighting off sleep and getting ready, make sure to take a couple of minutes and pray with your daughter. You can use the following Pre-Episode Prayer or pray on your own. I recommend praying before you head out the door.

Pre-Episode Prayer

Heavenly Father,

As _____ (daughter's name) and I embark on our adventure this morning, please help us to focus on You and Your Glory. We thank You for this morning and for our time together enjoying Your canvas of colors in the morning sky. Guide us today as we explore our faith in You! I pray that _____'s (daughter's name) heart is stirred by Your Word, Your creation, and that we develop a deeper and more meaningful relationship as we look to discover and choose a Life Word or Life Verse to focus on knowing You better.

In Jesus' name we pray,
Amen

3-2-1 Action! Activity
As you and your daughter are viewing the eastern skies, ask your daughter this question:

Do you ever worry that the sun won't rise each morning?

Most likely, she will answer, "No." Then follow up with the best question in the world, *"Why?"*

This one might throw her off. She might answer with, "just because," "I don't know," or may even give you a detailed scientific answer. No matter her answer, be patient and listen.

Once she is completely done searching for an answer or explaining her answer, go ahead and read her the following Bible verses:

> *The Lord's unfailing love and mercy still continue,*
> *Fresh as the morning, as sure as the sunrise.*
> *The Lord is all I have, and so in him I put my hope.*
>
> Lamentations 3:22–24 (GNT)

> *Let us acknowledge the Lord; let us press on to acknowledge him. As surely as the sun rises, he will appear; he will come to us like the winter rains, like the spring rains that water the earth.*
>
> Hosea 6:3

Next, ask her the following question:

> *Do you believe that God controls the sun? When it rises and when it sets? Why or why not?*

Always encourage her answers. Continue to ask her questions that go deeper. Be prepared to share your belief, your faith, and your understanding of God's control of sunrises.

Then, be silent as the sun begins to creep above the horizon. Silently pray that the Holy Spirit works in your daughter's heart and soul as the beauty of His canvas spreads throughout the skies.

After a few minutes, break the silence and *ask your daughter to describe the sunrise: the colors, the beauty, and how it makes her feel.*

As you drink your hot cocoa and nibble on your blueberry or banana-nut muffin, explain to your daughter why you chose watching a sunrise for today's "Believe" Episode.

I encourage you to explain it from the heart, but feel free to use the following sample script:

"Today's 'Believe' Episode is all about faith. Just as Lamentations states: '*Fresh as the morning, as sure as the sunrise. The Lord is all I have, and so in him I put my hope.*' Each morning, we have faith that the sun will surely rise. I admit, I take it for granted. For that reason, I wanted to share today's sunrise with you to show you God's promise to you and to me. God is a faithful God, _____ (daughter's name).

Every color, every cloud, every ray of light is God's creation. He loves you. He believes in you. He has an amazing plan for you, _____ (daughter's name)! I know that you might be struggling with having faith in someone you can't see with your own eyes, something you can't feel with your fingers, or something you can't hear with your own ears. But each morning, God paints the sky for you as a reminder of His unending love for you.

So, when you struggle with your faith, aren't sure whether or not God hears you, or if He cares about you, I want you to remember this morning, this sunrise, and know that God is a faithful God.

To help commemorate and seal this morning's sunrise experience, you and your daughter will begin the process of choosing your very own "My One Word."

But wait, I don't even know what "My One Word" is. No problem. According to Pastor Michael Ashcraft, co-author of the book, *My One Word*, it is one word that "will give you a simple but effective plan to effect personal change (spiritual formation) by allowing a single word to become the lens through which you examine your heart and life for an entire year."[2]

He and his co-author, Rachel Olsen, go on to state, "It is better to do something about one thing than nothing about everything."[2]

The process is rather simple, but the exercise and adherence to focusing on your one word can be transformative. What an awesome way to help lead your daughter to Christ, to help her strengthen her faith, and to develop a deeper relationship with your little girl that is turning into a young woman right before your eyes.

Here are the four simple steps that Ashcraft, Olsen, and I have developed to help you and your daughter to choose your "My One Word:"

Choose just one word that represents what you most hope God will do in you, and focus on it for an entire year.

1. Determine the kind of person you want to become.[2]

   It must dive deep into your soul, the condition of your heart, and what you believe God created you to be.

2. Identify the characteristics of that person you want to become.[2]

   What are the qualities of the person you want to become?

3. Pick a word.[2]

   Once you have your list of characteristics, pick one word and commit to only one.

4. LaMaster's additional step: Write down each of your "My One Words" on a sheet of paper with the date and sign it.

You can do this on any piece of paper or check out The *Friday Night Light for Fathers and Daughters* One Word Certificate at MarkLaMaster.com/oneword

To help get you brainstorming, here are The Top Ten Most-Often-Picked Words, according to Mike Ashcraft:

1. Trust

2. Patience

3. Love

4. Discipline

5. Focus

6. Faith

7. Surrender

8. Peace

9. Listen

10. Joy[2]

My One Word (Dad): _____

Brief Explanation: _____
_____
_____
_____

My One Word (Daughter): _____

Brief Explanation: _____
_____
_____
_____

✦ Backstage Pass

Before you leave the location, ask your daughter the following questions:

1. Would you say that you have a strong faith in God?

2. How can I help you in your faith walk?

3. What is your biggest struggle with your faith right now? Can you tell me more about it?

4. Do you have any questions for me about my faith?

Before you begin your Red Carpet Interview, take a few moments to share your faith journey and/or testimony with your daughter.

♙ Red Carpet Interview

Now it's time for the bright lights, red carpet, and flashing cameras!

Get out your smartphone, put it in video mode, and hand it to your daughter. It's your turn to answer the questions.

Red Carpet Questions for Dad

1. What did you enjoy most about the sunrise this morning? Why?

2. What did you learn about me and my faith today?

3. What might you do when you are struggling with your faith?

4. Tell me your "My One Word" and why you chose it.

Red Carpet Questions for Daughter

1. What was your favorite part about today's "Believe" Episode? Why?

2. What was one thing you learned about me and my faith today?

3. What "My One Word" did you choose and why?

4. How many popcorn buckets would you give today's Episode? (Circle your choice)

 **Hannah's Take**

When I first thought about choosing My One Word, I was overwhelmed that I would have to keep it forever! I want you to know that it is all right to change your My One Word throughout different times of your life, your school year, or even every year.

For example, I started last year off with My One Word being *courage* and have since changed it to *trust*. The whole point of choosing a word is to help guide you toward God, not to stress you out about finding the perfect word.

—Hannah

Reminder: I invite you to the *Friday Night Lights for Fathers Private Facebook Group* to share your Episode experiences.

Inside of this Private Facebook Group, you will be able to share pictures and videos from each Episode with other dads and daughters. You can also ask questions, get new ideas, and connect with other dads from across the country. I look forward to seeing you inside soon!

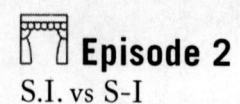 **Episode 2**　　　　**Date:** ____ / ____ / _____
S.I. vs S-I

Episode Guide

Theme
Body Confidence

"SCRIPT"-ure

All beautiful you are, my darling; there is no flaw in you.
Song of Songs 4:7

Set Location
Grocery Store and Home Kitchen

3-2-1 Action! Activity
Baking your favorite pie

The Pitch

$1 Billion
1 million
10%
$35 million
$10 million
54
46
0.000000013%

These numbers make absolutely no sense right now, but believe me, they will shock you. Any guesses? No cheating by reading ahead!

I will get to the numbers in a minute, but first, I want to give you a quick overview of the topic of today's Episode.

This Episode covers one of the most critical emotional topics your daughter will encounter during her adolescence—self-image.

I was just recently reminded how impactful self-image is to a 13-year-old girl. We spent a perfect summer day at a lake with my sister's family. Her 14-year-old daughter brought two of her close friends to partake in the summer fun. Only six months and one grade level apart, Hannah was introduced to her cousin's friends. It seemed to be going well—until it was time to get ready to go swimming.

Hannah was so excited to go swimming, boating, and going down the inflatable slide with her brother, her cousins, and her cousin's friends. She snuck off to the bathroom to change into her modest, one-piece swimsuit and waited patiently for the others to get changed.

Within a few minutes, the three 14-year-olds met up with Hannah in their more revealing two-piece bikinis. Jen and I could immediately tell that Hannah was uncomfortable in her own suit and own body.

To be clear, I am not preaching legalism and stating that all teenage girls must wear modest, one-piece bathing suits. On the contrary, I am making the point that teenage girls look at other girls' bodies and compare themselves, just as us guys naturally compare our dad bods. Your daughter has likely or will soon encounter a similar situation, and I want to help prepare you for it.

The cousins and friends went on to have a blast in the lake on that perfect summer day. I made a point to talk to Hannah about how she was feeling. It was just a couple of minutes, but I wanted her to know I loved her, I was proud of her, and that she was created perfectly by her Creator, God.

As if God had known this situation would be coming

soon (I know He planned it), I had just read *Every Young Woman's Battle*, by Shannon Ethridge and Stephen Arterburn, as part of my research for this book.

The authors describe how a young woman with a troubled past and poor sense of body image found comfort in the following verse, today's "SCRIPT"-ure:

All beautiful you are, my darling; there is no flaw in you.
Song of Songs 4:7

This young woman then wrote the following note:

God thinks I'm beautiful! The Creator of the Universe who hung the sun, moon, and stars calls me beautiful! I never realized how powerful those words are. If God spoke and the world was created, then His word is power. If God said, "Let there be light," and there was, then if He says I'm beautiful, then I am. It may take me a while to see myself this way, but God said it and that makes it true. If God thinks I'm beautiful, then I guess what other people think doesn't really matter.[1]

If you don't have your daughter do anything else with this Episode other than read this young woman's testimony and Song of Songs 4:7, you will be doing her a great service.

Whether or not the young woman who wrote the above note knew it or not, she, with God's help, had started a transition from being body conscious to becoming body confident.

According to Magali Amadei and Claire Mysko, founders of *Inside Beauty*:

Body confidence is the belief that you are your most beautiful when you are healthy—both in body and mind. A feeling that results when you give up the mission to mold and shape yourself and make a commitment to take care of yourself. Body confidence breeds positive body image—it enables us to see ourselves through a meaningful lens, not a superficial one.[2]

As I continued to research body confidence, I came across one of my all-time favorite author's definitions. In her recent book, *Raising Body-Confident Daughters*, Dannah Gresh eloquently intertwines God in her definition of body confidence:

"Body-confidence is the state of knowing your body's purpose and being able to depend on it to do what God designed it to do without making too much or too little of it."[3]

She goes on to give these nuggets of truth about body confidence:

On a pendulum, it [body confidence] is located somewhere in the middle of caring enough but not too much. How can this delicate balance be achieved? This may surprise you, but teaching your daughter to confidently care about her body in a godly way doesn't even start with a focus on her body! It starts with an "emphasis on the care of her spirit and teaching her to press in to godliness."The road to body confidence starts with being more concerned with the spirit than the body.[3]

So, dads, how can we teach our daughters to "press into godliness" and help build up our daughters' body confidence?

If you have participated in one of my online video coaching programs, you know that I love to use video clips to help emphasize my teaching points. I couldn't think of a better time to inject a YouTube clip that will illustrate the lies both our daughters and ourselves are being fed through the beauty culture of advertising.

Type in the following website address and watch the

following 1-minute video, titled Body Evolution: https://youtu.be/17j5QzF3kqE

My hope is that this 1-minute video clip gives you an inside perspective on how much time, resources, and effort go into making the models we see in advertisements everywhere look "perfect."

In her book, *Digital Media: Human Technology Connection*, author Stacey O'Neal Irwin writes, "Studies show that close to 100% of all published images in the main-stream media are photoshopped . . ."[4]

If almost all images are photoshopped or digitally re-touched, the images our daughters are seeing are not realistic, and this culture's definition of beauty will always be unattainable in their eyes unless we help them understand what true beauty is.

Who can blame our daughters' struggles with their body image? Let's look at one more example to illustrate our culture's craving for the perfect body.

Remember all of those numbers I had you read at the beginning of the Episode? Well, here is what they represent. (If any of your guesses related to the *Sports Illustrated* Swimsuit Issue (SISI), you get bonus points!).

$1 billion: The estimated collective revenue from the SI swimsuit edition since debuting in 1964.[5]

1 million: The number of *Sports Illustrated* Swimsuit Editions sold on newsstands alone annually (about 10 to 15 times as much as regular issues).[5]

10%: The percent of revenue *Sports Illustrated* generates exclusively from the Swimsuit Edition.[6]

$35 million: The estimated revenue from the swimsuit issue alone in 2005. Think of what it is now![6]

$10 million: The amount of increased annual income from the *Sports Illustrated* Swimsuit Calendar, video and TV specials, trading cards, screen savers, and other secondary products.[5]

55: Number of Swimsuit Editions as of 2018 since its first issue in 1964.

47: Number of models who have graced the cover of a *Sports Illustrated* Swimsuit Edition.

0.000000013%: The percentage of women in the world that have earned a spot on the cover of the *Sports Illustrated* Swimsuit Edition. (Based on world population of 7.5 billion and 50% women.)

Do these numbers surprise you? Which number(s) caught you off guard the most? For me, it was 1 million issues sold and the fact that one annual swimsuit issue has been able to generate $1 billion over the course of its lifetime.

In order to keep the readers interested though, the editors have had to spice things up a bit. In 2014, Hannah Davis' cover, I believe, crossed the line between appropriate and inappropriate. I am not the only one—a *Washington Post* writer asked if the cover goes "too low" with Davis' bikini bottom and received many comments like "Horrible message for young girls" and "They should change the name to *Sports Illustrated* Playboy edition."[7] In a *Us Weekly* poll, 68% of readers thought the cover image resembled porn, while 38% found it "so hot!"[8]

I agree that recent covers are sending a horrible message for our daughters, especially knowing that all of the cover models' photos are airbrushed, photoshopped, or retouched in some way, shape, or form (much like the above YouTube video).

I encourage you to share all of this information with your daughter during the course of the "S.I. vs. S-I" Episode. The more truth she knows, the more she will become comfortable in her uniqueness and know that she has a loving earthly father and heavenly Father.

Now, let's find out how we need to prepare for this Episode.

Behind the Scenes Setup (for Dad)

Set Location

No problem with the set location today because the majority of the activities will take place in your own kitchen. A portion of today's Episode will also take place at your local grocery store.

3-2-1 Action! Activity Overview

As you go through today's activity, you will be focusing on building up your daughter's self-image and body confidence, reminding her that God has created her without one single flaw and that true beauty comes from the inside.

When my daughter was five or six years old, we would watch The Food Network together. I know, not the best educational material to fill her young mind with, but she absolutely loved it. She especially liked it when they baked pies. Hannah and I often baked in those days, including, cookies, bars, and homemade pies.

To help illustrate these concepts, you will need to put your baker's hat on for this Episode. That's right—you and your daughter will be shopping for all of the ingredients and will spend some one-on-one time baking up a delicious pie.

Stage Checklist

- Schedule The Live Shoot! with your daughter and add it to your calendar.

- Together, decide what kind of pie you want to bake and make sure you find a recipe for it. (I will share my Grandma K's Blushing Apple Pie recipe below).

- Make a shopping list for the ingredients and pick up a pie pan if you don't have one.

- Don't forget the fixin's: vanilla ice cream, whipped cream (the spray kind, of course), milk, and coffee.

- If you are more of a semi-homemade baker, feel free to purchase pre-made crusts (it's about the experience, not whether or not you can roll out a pie crust).

- Print a copy of the image of the pie you decide to bake.

Great Grandma K's Blushing Apple Pie Recipe

Apple Mixture:

> **6 cups** pared, sliced apples (Hannah and I like Golden Delicious apples the best)
> **1 cup** sugar depending on the tartness of the apples
> **4–5 rounded tbsp.** flour depending on the juiciness of the apples
> **2 tbsp.** butter—cut and dabbed on top before putting on top crust or lattice
> Brush with melted butter and sprinkle sugar on top of crust
> ¼ **cup** Red Hots candies

Crust:
> **1 cup** flour
> **2 rounded tbsp.** lard or Crisco
> *Note: Makes one 9" crust, so make sure to double this*
>
> OR
>
> **2 pre-made pie crusts** (gluten-free options are available).

If you are up for a bit more of challenge, make a lattice crust topping. It takes a bit more time, but will add a bit more to your experience.

Using the crust for the top of the pie, cut it into twelve 1-inch-wide strips. Arrange 6 strips across the pie. Form the lattice by arranging 6 strips diagonally across the first 6 strips. Then, gently press ends into crust edges. Brush the lattice with milk. Sprinkle lightly with additional sugar.

Finally, bake pie in oven for 50 minutes or until crust is golden brown.

🎥 The Live Shoot!

It's almost time to head to the grocery store and pick up all of the ingredients for your very own homemade pie. Before you head out the door, pray with your daughter and ask that God would bless your time together.

Pre-Episode Prayer

Heavenly Father,

Your Word tells us that You "created all of the delicate, inner parts of our bodies and knit us together in our mother's womb." (Psalm 139:13) Despite knowing this, we often struggle with our self-image and compare ourselves with others. Help _____ (daughter's name) and me better understand that You created us in Your image without flaws. Our culture constantly causes us to feel that we are not good enough, pretty enough, tall enough, cute enough, and on and on. During today's Episode, help me to show _____ (daughter's name) that she is beautiful just the way You created her and help her to look to You for comfort when the culture is cruel.

In Jesus' name we pray,
Amen

3-2-1 Action! Activity

On your way to the grocery store, have your daughter read through The Pitch with a special focus on the definitions of body confidence. Then have her read the "SCRIPT"-ure aloud, and let her know that you will talk more about it later.

Set 1—The Grocery Store

As you walk through the grocery store and choose your ingredients, make sure to compare a few of the name brand items and the store brand items. Often, the store brands have the exact same ingredients as the national brands, and the only thing that is different is the packaging and the price.

Ask your daughter which item she thinks you should buy and why. If she answers because it is cheaper, congratulations dad, you have a savvy buyer and have raised her well. Most likely though, your daughter will be like most of the rest of us and choose the item with the more attractive label.

You can then explain to her that companies spend millions of dollars in marketing research to create the most appealing label so that potential customers will choose their brand. Typically, this is why the national brand costs more than the store brand that does little or no marketing.

Finish up your shopping list and make sure not to forget the vanilla ice cream and Red Hots (if you are using Grandma K's recipe).

Set 2—The Kitchen

Now that you are back home, have the baking supplies unloaded, and are ready to start baking, show your daughter a picture of the pie you want to make. It should be included in the recipe, but if not, go ahead and search the Internet for a picture of it.

If it is from the Internet or a magazine, it will look absolutely perfect and most likely, photoshopped or retouched in some way. Talk about whether or not you and your daughter think you can make one that looks exactly like the one in the photo. Why or why not?

Next talk about the ingredients. Did you buy the national or store brand? Ask your daughter if she thinks the brand of ingredients will make any difference in how the pie turns out? Why?

Once you both have a good idea of how the pie is supposed to turn out, get baking! Let your daughter do the majority of the work. While you are baking, don't forget to take a few fun and goofy action shots to show the before and after.

Once you have put the pie in the oven, do the dishes together and make sure the kitchen is cleaner than you found it.

Next, find a place that the two of you can talk alone without interruption from other family members. After doing the dishes, you should have at least 30 minutes before the pie is done baking.

🎟 Backstage Pass

Make sure to take advantage of this part of the Episode and ask your daughter the following questions about self-image and body confidence.

It might be hard to get the conversation started with this topic, so you could start out by saying something like this:

_____ (daughter's name), I know that talking about your self-image is something that might be easier to talk to about with your mother or another woman, but I want you to know that you can always talk to me about it, too.

OR

As I was reading through this Episode, I realized how important it is that dads talk to their daughters about their self-image. Are you all right if I ask you a few questions about it?

1. Do you have any questions about body confidence and self-image?

2. What are three things you like about the way you look?

3. Is there anything you are concerned about with your body?

4. Do you believe that God created you flawlessly? Why or why not?

5. Has anyone ever bullied you about your body? Can you tell me more about it?

6. What part of you makes you feel most insecure? Why?

If you are in a deep conversation with your daughter when the timer on the oven goes off, take a moment to take the pie out of the oven, but then get right back and continue the conversation.

When you feel comfortable that you have answered all of your daughter's questions, make sure to tell you that you love her and that she is beautiful. Remind her that she was created perfectly and flawlessly created by God.

Speak from your heart. Your daughter craves your words and will always remember them. If you need a little inspiration to get you started, here is an example:

You are perfectly made, _____ (daughter's name)! I love you so much and am so proud of the young woman you are becoming. I am so blessed to have the opportunity to be your Dad.

Head out to the kitchen and take a look at the pie that you created, maybe even take a picture of it.

Ask your daughter a few more questions:

Does our pie look as perfect as the one in the picture? (unless you are a professional pie maker, her answer will be "kind of" or "no way.")

But we followed the directions exactly! Why didn't it turn out as perfect as the one in the picture?

Dads, here is where to bring the whole Episode together. This is where you can help your daughter apply all that you have learned together today to real life.

_____ (daughter's name), even though we used all of the same ingredients as the one in the picture, our pie is unique in its own way. Our crust is one-of-a-kind. Our filling has all been baked together to create the perfect balance of sweet and tart. Our pie was baked in the oven for just the right amount of time. Our pie is delicious and wonderful just as it is. I wouldn't want it any other way.

In just the same way, God created you to be wonderful just the way you are. He used just the right ingredients and knit you together in your mother's womb. He knew you before He formed you (Jeremiah 1:5). Everything about you was perfectly created by your Heavenly Father. We are all made from the same ingredients, but know that "you are beautiful and there is no flaw in you." I love you, _____ (daughter's name), and I am so proud of the young woman you are becoming.

Now, go enjoy some pie and ice cream while you hit the Red Carpet!

🎬 Red Carpet Interview

Red Carpet Questions for Dad

1. Dad, be honest, how do you think our pie turned out?

2. Have you ever bought a *Sports Illustrated* Swimsuit Issue? Why?

3. What did you learn about me today that you didn't know before?

4. Dad, did you ever struggle with your self-image or body confidence when you were my age? Tell me more about it.

5. When do you want to bake a pie with me again?

Red Carpet Questions for Daughter

1. What is one thing that you learned about body confidence today?

2. Does it help to know that God knew you before you were born and created you flawlessly? Explain?

3. What can I do to help you with your self-image and body confidence?

4. What was your favorite part about today's Episode? Why?

5. How many popcorn buckets would you give today's Episode? (Circle your choice)

Hannah's Take

You can still wear nice clothes, cute outfits, and look great, yet remain modest. In other words, you can have body confidence without wearing clothes that are too revealing.

Remember, God loves you no matter what brand-name you wear, how you look, or how popular you are—He just wants you to put Him first. Dressing modestly is one way we can honor Him.

—Hannah

Join *Friday Night Lights for Fathers Private Facebook Group* and share a picture of your homemade pie!

Episode 3 Date: ____ / ____ / _____
Friends vs. Frenemies

 **Episode Guide**

Theme
Godly Friendships

"SCRIPT"-ure

"A sweet friendship refreshes the soul."
Proverbs 27:9 MSG

Set Location
Local Shopping Mall

3-2-1 Action! Activity
Shopping Excursion

📢 The Pitch

Sugar and spice
and everything nice
that's what little girls are made of

Sunshine and rainbows
and ribbons for hair bows
that's what little girls are made of

Tea parties, laces
and baby doll faces
that's what little girls are made of

—Author Unknown

Somewhere between our daughters' birth and their teenage years, the "Sugar and Spice" sweetness often sours, can turn bitter, and often spoils. Why? A loaded question for sure, and I don't claim to know the answer. However, one contributing factor to the sugar-spoiling effect is certainly our daughters' friendship journey.

Many of our friends warned Jen and me that 6th grade was the year that everything changes for girls—cliques form, drama ensues, and mean girls emerge. For Hannah, 6th grade was a breeze, with only a little drama here and there.

As a brother growing up with two sisters, I thought I had seen almost every mean and manipulative trick girls could do to each other—and until my daughter turned 13, I felt comfortable and effective at fathering her through the few issues that surfaced. Whether it was being excluded from birthday party invites or sleepovers or who sits by whom on the bus, Jen and I were confident in handling the fairly infrequent issues.

We should have seen it coming during the summer before our daughter started 7th grade. Friends had been forming alliances right in front of our eyes. Then, before the year even started, Hannah joined a fall sport. Having no experience in the sport, we encouraged Hannah to try new things. As parents, we were proud of her for her going outside of her comfort zone, having no expectations of what would soon follow.

Hannah ended up making the varsity high school team. Hannah went to practice, was disciplined in her training, and maintained her position on varsity for the rest of the season. This is where we learned that personal success promotes jealously from insecure and immature peers. We thought it was athletics only but soon realized that it was academic performance, friendship circles, and beyond.

Ironically, it was not the upperclassmen that were jealous of Hannah's performance. In fact, they were supportive, encouraging, and even sweet to our sweetheart. Rather, it was one of her "friends." In our parenting naiveté, Jen and I encouraged Hannah to "shower her friend with kindness." We prayed that the issue would soon resolve. Hannah remained steadfast in her kindness approach, but continued to come home in tears caused by her friend.

Hannah completed her season as a 7th grader, was excelling academically, balancing honors classes and a varsity sport as a 13-year-old. Jen and I knew this was a lot for her to handle, but she thrived in it, she was energized by it—she was more confident than we had ever seen her.

Several of her friends were going to go out for a winter sport, a sport they encouraged her to go out for. Hannah was excited to again try something new. She couldn't wait to start, to get her equipment, her uniform, and find out what it all entailed.

Little did we know that on orientation night, the jealousy and competition would elevate to the next level, this time involving the friend's parent! I have never experienced an encounter with an adult as I did that night. It was as if this parent of Hannah's friend had seen a ghost. Instead of responding to a cordial, "How are you guys doing?", I received a stare that cut right through me. It was the look that said, "This is my daughter's sport, and your daughter doesn't belong here—how dare you show your face here!" We were standing directly in front of each other, amidst the other 200 athletes and parents who were excited for the season to start.

His daughter looked over at him, expecting him to say something back to me. He never did. He purposely held his stare for another painstaking second, then walked off into the crowd of people.

The poison was released, parent-to-parent, directly in front of our daughters, still friends at the time. I couldn't believe what had just happened. Hannah knew what was happening, but we held our discussion until the car ride home.

Even though we tried not to let our little encounter affect our excitement of the evening, it did. On our car ride home, Hannah asked me, "Was that the weirdest and most awkward moment ever?"

Even the eyes of a 13-year-old could see the immaturity of this grown man, completely wrapped up in his dreams for his daughter's future athletic success. It was as if this man already had several athletic scholarships in mind for his daughter—and my daughter was a threat.

At this next level of jealousy and envy, fully involving the friend and her parents, Hannah marched on. As she marched on, her friend added many other mean girl tactics to her manipulation repertoire—glares, hair flips, whispers, back turns, and eventually rumor spreading. But the most significant strategy Hannah's friend possessed was her ability to hold onto her friend status.

Unfortunately, the nightly tears continued, no matter what parenting tactic Jen and I passed on to Hannah. Can I be honest with you for a moment, dads? I have never felt so angry and so helpless all at once. I went to my parents for advice. Both of my sisters had mean girl journeys of their own. Jen and I prayed for guidance, for continued strength for Hannah, for some relief of the constant torment this friend was targeting towards our sweet little daughter.

We were way past the "shower her with kindness" strategy. We had Hannah try to implement the tolerate and "this too shall pass" technique. We also had, to no avail, attempted the avoidance tactic. Then, we had success—we tried the "pursue other friendships" tactic. Hannah started spreading her wings, intentionally developing other friendships with other girls at her lunch table, in her other classes, and at church.

For a few weeks, things seemed to settle down for Hannah. The tearful nights were slowly being replaced with the sugar and spice and all that's nice about Hannah that we had always known.

But then . . .

But then, Hannah's friend made her next move. Her friend had become jealous of Hannah's newly formed friendships. Slowly but surely, she must have been plotting her plan to invade these new girls with her charming and conniving ways. She started subtly and progressed to rumor spreading, ignoring, and the silent treatment. She was smart enough to try to entrap Hannah in her games, but Hannah could see right through her schemes.

One of Hannah's newer friends had confided in Hannah that her friend had been saying how "mean," "clingy," and "annoying" Hannah had been to her, how she always made her feel left out, how she ignored her—all completely untrue.

Another night of tears and talking ensued. Hannah had finally had enough. She went to bed, both physically and emotionally exhausted. As usual, she woke up the next morning and completed her morning routine of Bible reading, devotions, and prayer, and got ready for school.

During the car ride to school that morning, Hannah said something that I will never forget. She said, "I am going to talk to her today, Dad. I am going to ask her why she has been acting like she has for so long. I am going to ask her to apologize to me in front our lunch table friends." I must have waited a bit too long for my response because Hannah had to say, "Dad . . . Dad . . . what do you think?"

I told her how mature I thought she was. I told her I was proud of her. I told her that I would pray for her throughout the day.

As she grabbed her overstuffed teal backpack and her flute, she said, "I love you, Dad," as she shut the door and headed into school. I was a bit stunned, mostly because I didn't know if I would have had the courage to confront the person that had caused me so much emotional pain.

When I picked Hannah up from school that afternoon, I was so nervous for Hannah. I wondered if she had confronted her friend or not. I was curious to find out how she felt about it. So, as she came down the sidewalk to the car, I whispered one final prayer.

On the drive home, Hannah told me she did, in fact, confront her friend. Her friend finally, but somewhat hesitantly, admitted her behavior and apologized. In my eyes, Hannah just made the varsity team again, but this time it was for the "relationship team." Jen and I were so proud of her and were so hopeful that things would only get better from here.

All three of us were wrong. Her friend faked all of us out for about a week but just couldn't keep from targeting Hannah and her continued success, her friendships, and her innocence.

As a dad, I knew what I wanted to do. Wasn't it my job to fix things, take care of issues, and make everything all right again? I felt stuck, handcuffed, and confused as to what to do. I could talk to the school counselor, the parents, or perhaps, even the principal. Jen and I had come to the end of our parenting knowledge and needed help.

So, I looked through the father and son parenting books I had researched for my first book, *Friday Night Lights for Fathers and Sons*, but didn't find anything that was remotely helpful for fathering my daughter through her friendship journey. I jumped online and began researching raising teen daughter books.

I singled out a book by Rachel Simmons, titled, *Odd Girl Out*. The subtitle is what truly captured my attention: *The*

Hidden Culture of Aggression in Girls. I started reading the book immediately—everything about Hannah's friend was making sense. With each page I turned, I gained insight into the manipulative mind of this teenaged girl.

As I finished page 20 and started in on page 21, I learned of three types of aggressive behavior I had never heard of before—definitions that fully described the techniques that Hannah's friend had been perfecting for the past year. Terms that Jen and I could finally put a name to, to learn about, and to parent from.

These three definitions have literally been a game-changer for Jen, Hannah, and I. Here's why—Simmons explains that a small group of psychologists at the University of Minnesota identified three types of aggressive behavior among girls.

The three types of aggressive behavior are:

1. *Relational aggression*: includes acts that harm others through damage (or the threat of damage) to relationships or feelings of acceptance, friendship, or group inclusion. Relationally aggressive behavior is ignoring someone to punish them or get one's own way, excluding someone socially for revenge, using negative body language or facial expressions, sabotaging someone else's relationships, or threatening to end a relationship unless the friend agrees to a request. In these acts, the aggressor uses her relationship with the target as a weapon.[1]

2. *Indirect aggression*: allows the aggressor to avoid confronting her target. It is covert behavior in which the aggressor makes it seem as though there has been no intent to hurt at all. One way this is possible is by using others as vehicles for inflicting pain on a targeted person, such as spreading a rumor.[1]

3. *Social aggression*: is intended to damage the
   self-esteem or social status within a group . . . including social exclusion.[1]

Whether Hannah's friend knew it or not, she was guilty
of all three types of aggressive behavior, all directed at
my daughter. I believe she knew it. I also believe she had
learned it.

We now had definitions of the tactics this teenager was
tormenting our daughter with. We were comforted by the
fact that our daughter wasn't the only one being victimized
by middle school aggression. Unfortunately, we were still
unsure about how to parent Hannah through this struggle.

Within one academic year, our sugar and spice daughter
had experienced just the opposite. Here is an anonymous
12-year-old girl's updated rendition of the Sugar and
Spice poem:

> A shake of the head, a roll of the eyes
> The rumors the lies
> They no longer play on your pride
> But rip you up inside
> This is what girls do
> This is what they say
> It is like this every day . . .
> Walking in the hall
> Taking in it all . . .
> Kids shouting, kids staring
> All this torture I'm bearing
> No one caring[2]

As I continued to research more about girls who become
experts at relational, indirect, and social aggression, I ran
across the term "frenemy." Lisa Darmour, Ph.D., defines
frenemy as "a peer who is lots of fun except when she's being

completely rotten."[3] Darmour, author of *Untangled: Guiding Teenage Girls Through the Seven Transitions in Adulthood*, goes on to say:

> If your daughter has a frenemy, you probably won't hear much about the friendship when things are going well. But when your daughter's frenemy turns on her, you might learn about behavior that is surprisingly nasty.[3]

As dads, we want so badly to march right over to our daughter's frenemy and tell her to "knock it off . . . or else!" Obviously, this is not the right approach, but it has crossed my mind more often than I am willing to admit.

How then, are we to parent our daughter through what Darmour labels a "frenemyship?" Darmour, an experienced clinical psychologist who specializes in teen girl relationships, suggests we give our daughters the following advice:

1. "It's really up to you whether you keep hanging out with her. If you do, be careful when she's being nice because you know that may not last."

2. "We love you and hate seeing you put yourself in a position where you keep getting hurt."

3. "It sounds like she can be fun—I see why you guys hang out so much. But real friends don't do such mean things to each other."[3]

Perhaps the most enlightening (and frustrating) bit of advice Darmour has for dads is:

> It's unrealistic for parents to try to prevent an adolescent friendship . . . and, as tricky as a frenemy can be, it may be even trickier for girls to break off the friendship. Adolescent tribes are held together by complex social webs, and

a girl who cuts herself off from one peer may lose several friendships, or even an entire tribe.[3]

Darmour's advice has proven to be true time and time again. Our daughters understand this concept better than we do. The "complex social web" our daughters are immersed in is a world that we can't quite comprehend.

Before I go on any further, I want to ask you a couple of questions:

1. Can you name five of your daughter's friends?

2. Do you know your daughter's best friend's name? Last name?

3. Does your daughter have a frenemy? How do you know?

4. How are you currently parenting her when it comes to the topic of friendships?

5. Do you leave all of this girl friendship stuff to your wife, your daughter's mother, or any other mother figure?

The reason I ask these questions is because I hope it helps you realize how involved or not involved you are in this area of your daughter's life. If you answered "No" to questions 1–4 and "Yes" to question 5, you need to get in the game, dad!

For those of you that answered "Yes" to a few of the questions 1–4 and "No" to question 5, you realize that the role of the father has a great impact on your daughter's emotional development.

All of us dads must realize that getting to know more about our daughter's friendship world is not a one-time question and answer session. Your daughter wants you to know her friends, approve of her friends, and understand why she is friends with them—even though you are likely to get an eye roll or two.

So, how can we let our daughter know that we are interested in her friendships and learn more about her frenemies? By asking her the right questions.

How do we help lead her to godly friends? We define friendships the best way we know how, through the Bible, and we pray for her to develop godly friends.

Up until now, we have defined what a frenemy is and what a frenemyship is. We have also discussed what tactics frenemies use to cause toxicity amongst their targets, but we have yet to define a godly friendship. Well, that is about to change—now.

I searched high and low for this definition, but it was so worth it. Tim Keller, in his sermon titled, "Friendship," laid out the four building blocks for true, godly friendships:

1. Constancy (Loves at all times, good and bad)

2. Carefulness (emotionally sensitive and connected)

3. Candor (truth-teller)

4. Counsel (transparent—reassuring and challenging when required)[4]

Here is that definition of godly friendship I want to share with you and for you to share with your daughter:

"A friend always lets you in (candor/counsel) and never lets you down (constancy/carefulness)."[4]

Simplified even further, "A friend always lets you in and never lets you down."[4]

Let's bring in the our "SCRIPT"-ure for today's Episode:

"A sweet friendship refreshes the soul."
(Proverbs 27:9 MSG)

Why this verse? Because this verse touches not only all four of the building blocks of godly friendship as described by Tim Keller, but is the exact opposite of the aggression, the manipulation, and the evil tactics that frenemies exude.

Friends should refresh our daughters' souls in their action, their love, their encouragement, and their truth-telling. These are the types of friendships I want to help cultivate for my daughter.

But how in the world can I teach her about being selective with her choices in friends amidst the social mazes, frenemies, cliques, and entitled culture we find ourselves in?

Behind the Scenes Setup (for Dad)

While I know that this is only the third Episode, is it all right if I confess something to you? This particular 3-2-1! Action Activity was the last portion of the book that I wrote. Honestly, I could not, for the life of me, come up with an activity in which us dads could help teach our daughters how to develop godly friendships.

I prayed about it. I looked at website after website and book after book on the topic of friendships. I wrote a couple of drafts, then deleted them. Picture me sitting at a typewriter, inserting a piece of paper, typing a few sentences, and then tearing the piece of paper out of the typewriter, crumpling it up, and then throwing it on the floor—you know the scene.

Then, I did what I should have done in the first place—I asked Hannah. She answered almost immediately as if she had been waiting for me to ask the question. Hannah's answer? "Shopping, of course."

I need to explain something to you, Hannah is not a typical teenage shopper. She doesn't ask to go shopping, she doesn't go shopping at the mall with her friends (yet), and she isn't a drama shopper.

One thing about her shopping that stands out though is that Hannah is an extremely picky shopper—especially when it comes to shopping for jeans. In her young life, she has only owned a couple of pairs of jeans. They are "too itchy" or "don't feel right" to her.

I am a Levi's 501 guy. I have bought several other brands of jeans, but know that 501's fit me the best, are the most comfortable, and last the longest. I have even tried other types of Levi's jeans, but I always end up going for the 501's.

I soon realized how choosing friends is a lot like shopping for a new pair of jeans.

Set Location
Your daughter's choice for jeans shopping—a local shopping mall or clothing store

3-2-1 Action! Activity Overview
When was the last time you went clothes shopping with your daughter? I mean, just the two of you. If you are at all like me, I somewhat despise shopping, so, for me, I honestly don't even remember the last time Hannah and I set out on a shopping excursion.

Well, it's about time to plan that father and daughter shopping trip. For today's Episode, you will be inviting your daughter on a shopping excursion—just the two of you.

Stage Checklist

1. Invite your daughter to go shopping for a pair of jeans. Make sure she chooses the mall or the stores where she wants to shop.

2. Confirm the date and put it on your calendar.

3. Share with your daughter that the theme of today's Episode is about godly friendships. Answer any questions she might have.

4. Before you begin your shopping excursion, re-read The Pitch and the Behind the Scenes Setup and refresh your memory on godly friendships versus frenemyships.

5. Give your daughter a spending limit in advance, so this does not become an opportunity for any disagreement later. Offer your daughter the option to use her own money to increase the amount of the cost of the jeans.

   - Feel free to replace jeans with any other article of clothing that your daughter wishes to purchase, just know that I will be using a pair of jeans for this activity.

   - Dad, the spending limit is up to you. Don't feel that you have to break the bank for this Episode.

🎥 The Live Shoot!

Hopefully, you have been building anticipation and excitement for today's Episode. Your daughter, whether or not she is a shopper or not, will undoubtedly enjoy spending one-on-one time with you.

Pre-Episode Prayer

Heavenly Father,

Today, _____ (daughter's name) and I ask you to join us as we explore godly friendships. Help us to understand how to develop refreshing and loving friendships rather than manipulative and conniving frenemyships. We look to

You to guide us today as we learn how to identify and pursue friends that will always let us in and never let us down. We know they exist. We know that there will be few, but we also trust that only You can help lead us to these types of friends. May Your Word, Your examples, and Your Spirit fill our conversation on cultivating godly friendships today.

In Jesus' name we pray,
Amen.

3, 2, 1, Action! Activity

Once you get to the mall or shopping center, find a place to sit down and talk.

Go ahead and take out this book and ask your daughter the following questions about shopping for her new pair of jeans:

1. What do you look for when choosing a pair of jeans? Why?

2. With all of the different kinds of jeans, how do you know which style or brand to choose?

3. Have you ever picked out "the perfect" jeans only to find out later that it didn't fit quite right, wasn't comfortable, or looked different when you tried it on at home?

4. Have you ever had a pair of jeans that you really didn't like become one of your favorites? Tell me about them.

5. When shopping for jeans, do you know right away that you they will become your favorite pair?

6. How long would you be willing to wait to find just the right pair of jeans?

Now that you both have a good idea about what style of jeans your daughter wants and a bit more about why she likes that particular kind, it's time to go shopping.

Go to your daughter's favorite store and head to the jeans section. Take a patience pill, like I have to, and wait for your daughter to try on a few pairs of jeans.

Be open to the possibility that she may not find a pair at this store. In fact, your daughter might not be able to find a pair of jeans at any store during today's Episode. No worries, it has happened to the best of us.

Whether or not your daughter finds a pair of jeans or not, you are still spending time together. Once your daughter has her pair of jeans or you have both decided to call it a day, find a place where you can grab a snack and something to drink. It's now time to connect the dots on friendship and to connect with your daughter about how to cultivate godly friendships.

🎟 Backstage Pass

We are going to start this Backstage Pass off with a BANG!—a rapid-fire list of questions for you to ask your daughter:

1. What is your best friend's name?

2. What about her makes her your best friend?

3. Do you know what a frenemy is?

   a. If so, do you have one? What's her name?

   b. If not, explain to her what a frenemy is.

4. If you have a frenemy, what kinds of things does she do that makes her a frenemy?

5. Name five people that you sit by at the lunch table at school.

6. What qualities make a good or bad friend?

7. Is it easy or hard for you to make friends? Why or why not?

8. Do you ever pray for your friends?

9. Do you ever pray for new friends?

10. Would it be all right if we talked more about your friendships or friend issues?

Dad, these are some tough questions, and a few of her answers may take you by surprise (especially #10).

You may have just learned a lot more about your daughter in the last few minutes than you did in the past few weeks or months. Way to go!

But now it's time to pull out the big guns. Ask your daughter the following questions and give her a couple of minutes to answer.

1. What do you look for when choosing your friends? Why?

2. With all of the different kinds of girls at school, how do you know how to choose the right friends?

3. Have you ever thought you picked out the perfect friend only to find out later that you were completely wrong?

4. Have you ever had a friend that you initially didn't like, but over time, you became good friends?

5. Do you believe that you can become friends with someone the first time you meet them? Why or why not?

6. How long are you willing to wait to find new friends or for a friendship to develop?

After she answers this question, pause for a moment, and ask:

7. Do you realize that I just asked you the same six questions about your friends and friendships that I asked you about finding the perfect pair of jeans?

Why? Because I want to help you understand that choosing your friends and cultivating friendships are like choosing your jeans—trying them on, wearing them, and being patient with them until they become your favorite pair of jeans.

Choosing your friends are like choosing the perfect pair of jeans. It takes time to get to know each other, but once you get to know them, you almost feel incomplete without them, they become part of you. Just like your favorite pair of jeans might have some stains, some holes, or some flaws over time, a friend, a godly friend will accept you for who you are, stains, holes, flaws, and all!

8. _____ (your daughter's name), can you give me your best definition of friendship?

That is a great definition, _____ (your daughter's name). Would you like if I shared with you a definition of a godly friendship?

"A friend always lets you in and never lets you down."[4]

My prayer for you is that this godly definition helps guide you throughout the course of your life as you make friends. Don't forget that "A sweet friendship refreshes the soul." Proverbs 27:9 (MSG)

🎬 Red Carpet Interview

Red Carpet Questions for Dad

1. Dad, what are your favorite kinds of jeans and why?

2. Who is your best friend and why?

3. Dad, can you say the first and last names of five of my friends or girls I hang out with?

4. Will you pray for me that I seek out and develop godly friends?

Red Carpet Questions for Daughter

1. _____ (daughter's name), what are your favorite kind of jeans and why?

2. Can you tell me the definition of a godly friendship that we talked about during today's Episode?

3. When you have friend "issues," do you know that I am here to listen and to help you through them?

4. What was one thing that you learned about friendships today?

5. How many popcorn buckets would you give today's Episode? (Circle your choice)

🎬 Hannah's Take

I have learned that true, godly friends stand by you through the good and bad. My dad told me a quote by Jim Rohn that

I want to share with you, "You are the average of the five people you spend the most time with."

When choosing friends or trying to figure out whether or not to continue a friendship, I always think about this quote. Not too long ago, I read Proverbs 12:26, "The righteous choose their friends wisely, but the way of the wicked leads them away." Pray about your friendships because God wants to guide us!

—Hannah

Have a cool pic of you and your daughter in your new pair of jeans? Share it in the *Friday Night Lights for Fathers Private Facebook Group* and join in on the fun.

🎬 Episode 4
Waffles and Wi-Fi

Date: ____ / ____ / _____

🎞 Episode Guide

Theme
Navigating the Social Media Maze

"SCRIPT"-ure

> *To act justly and to love mercy and to walk humbly with your God.*
>
> *Micah 6:8*

Set Location
Choose your favorite waffle restaurant and make sure it has free Wi-Fi.

3-2-1 Action! Activity
Co-write a set of Social Media Guardrails

📣 The Pitch

Dads, do you want to know what one of the most important decisions you will ever make in the life of your tween or teenage daughter is?

Take a moment to consider your answer. Think about the latest news reports, what you read in the paper, or the story your co-worker shared about his daughter.

When I ask this question to my readers, my clients, to audiences, and the dads I know, you can imagine what some of the answers might be. Want to know a few?

- When she should start dating

- When she should get a job

- What school she should attend

- What church your family should attend

- When to have "The Sex Talk" with her

- When to get her a smartphone

Certainly, these are all important decisions that we must make in conjunction with our wives or your daughter's mother. Now that you have your answer keep it at the front of your mind.

I promise I will share with you what I believe is the most important decision in the life of your tween or teenage daughter.

But before I do, I want to share a story with you. After reading this story, I believe you will have a few more clues as to what my answer might be. Ready?

Kelly, a 13-year-old 7th grader, came home with tears in her eyes. When her dad asked her if she wanted to talk about it, she said, "No, I just want to be by myself."

The dad waited about 30 minutes and then knocked on the door to her room. "Honey, I would really like to talk to you about what happened at school today." She invited him in and tried telling her story as she sobbed.

The dad could tell that she was terrified to tell him the truth, but it became obvious that she needed to let her shame out. It had been piling up for weeks now. She knew this moment would come, but she didn't want to disappoint her parents, especially her dad. Would he be mad? Would she get in trouble? Would he yell at her?

Her dad reassured her that he would listen to her without interrupting and that he cared about her, that he loved her, and that he was on her side.

Once Kelly was reassured, she revealed the cause of her tears.

About a month or so before, Kelly met a boy, a cute boy, Jake, on Snapchat. He said she was "gorgeous" and followed her. Soon, they couldn't get enough of each other. They would Snap each other first thing in the morning and the last thing before they fell asleep. Their "SnapStreak" was, "like, record-breaking!"

He would Snap her during school, before school, after school, during dinner, during activities, and any other time. She had to Snap him back. Kelly assumed that if she didn't, he wouldn't like her anymore.

Soon, they decided to meet up. Kelly admitted to her dad that she lied about going to her best friend's house a couple of weeks ago, and went to Jake's house instead. She also told her dad that his parents were not home, but she promised they "didn't do anything."

Kelly told her dad that she loved the attention that this cute boy was giving her. Jake kept telling her how "hot" she was, how much he loved her smile and her eyes. Everything seemed to be going well.

Until . . . he sent her the following text—"Send nOODz?"

For those of us that don't know what "nOODz" is, it means naked pictures of yourself.

Kelly knew it wasn't right. Her parents had taught her that selfies were "for faces only." She had texted her best friend for advice, and she told her to go for it.

Even though she knew it was wrong, she took a picture of her naked breasts and hit the send button. She completely trusted this cute guy, and besides, the Snap only lasts 10 seconds and then disappears.

Her boyfriend responded immediately with, "you are even more beautiful than I imagined!" It was like an adrenaline rush. Kelly felt on top of the world, "This cute guy thinks I'm hot."

All was going well until Kelly received another text request from her boyfriend about a week later: "Send full nOODz?"

Yes, this cute boyfriend was now asking for a full, completely nude picture of Kelly. Kelly thought things were going so well. He didn't share the picture of her breasts; he certainly wouldn't share the full shot.

So, with her 13-year old mindset, she locked her bedroom door, posed, clicked, and sent the full nude shot via Snapchat to her boyfriend.

Kelly knew that the relationship was getting more serious now. She couldn't wait to see Jake again. Having a boyfriend was the most exciting thing that had ever happened to her in her short life. Kelly imagined herself climbing up the popularity ladder at school, hanging out at the more popular lunch table, and making new friends with the popular girls—all because she had a boyfriend.

"So, today," Kelly continued to share her story with her dad, "I get to school, and everyone is looking at me like I'm like some kind of, like, freak! I knew something was wrong right away. I texted my best friend and asked her what was going on. She texted me back the full nude that I sent my boyfriend."

Jake had taken a screenshot of the Snap Kelly sent him, then sent it to a few of his friends and voila! It went viral throughout the school and beyond.

Through sobs, Kelly told her dad that the whole school now had her naked body on their phones. "Dad, what am I supposed to do? Jake won't even talk to me. His best friend told me that he didn't even like me. He just told me what I wanted to hear so he could collect as many nOOdz of girls as he could. He got more points for full nudes. Dad, I feel so used. I thought he would like me more if I sent him the pictures ... I trusted him. I hate myself. My life is ruined. ..."

According to Nancy Jo Sales, author of *American Girls: Social Media and the Secret Lives of Teenagers*, this story is happening in your city and your school system, today.

You might be thinking, *not my girl, not in my little town*, or *we have taught her about that already*. After reading *American Girls* and Sales' research, I certainly had a change of heart.

Sales spent two years researching *American Girls*, visiting ten states and interviewing over 200 girls, ages thirteen to nineteen, about their use of social media. She "spoke to girls from different socioeconomic backgrounds, of different races ... black, white, Latino, Asian, Asian Indian, and Native American." Sales goes on to state, "One of the things that continually struck me over the course of my reporting was the similarity of girls' experiences on social media regardless of their race or background ... the technology and widespread use of the same apps seem to be creating ... a certain culture."[1]

Well, you might say, "I will just talk with my daughter about this once, and she will listen to me. She's a great kid. I trust her."

This isn't one of those topics to sweep under the table dads. Sexting is one of those topics to tackle head on. If you are not yet sure what sexting is, it is the sending of sexually explicit digital images, videos, text messages, or emails, sent by cell phone.

According to Peggy Orenstein, author of *Girls and Sex: Navigating the Complicated New Landscape*, "between 15 and 48 percent (depending on the age of the children asked and how 'sexting' is defined) say they have sent or received an explicit text or photo." What's more concerning for us dads with daughters is that "girls are twice as likely to be among those who are pressured, coerced, blackmailed, or threatened into it."[2]

Jesse Weinberger, who wrote the smartphone and Internet safety book, *The Boogeyman Exists: And He's in Your*

Child's Back Pocket, said she had surveyed 70,000 children and found that, on average, sexting began in the fifth grade![3]

The Answer

Earlier, I asked you the following question:

> *Dads, do you want to know what one of the most important decisions you will ever make in the life of your tween or teenage daughter is?*

After reading Kelly's story and the recent research on the topic, would you agree that one of the most important decisions you will ever make in the life of your tween or teenage daughter is when to allow her to access social media?

Here are some social media platforms that you will need to familiarize yourself with. With all things technology, these will continue to change as quickly as Culver's "Frozen Flavor of the Day," so I encourage you to stay up-to-date with the changes.

As of April 2017, Instagram holds a slight lead in the battle for the top social media platform for girls aged 13–17 at 59.6%. In a close second, Snapchat comes in at 56.4%. Following a bit behind is Facebook (52.8%), Google (42.2%), Twitter (35.4%), and Pinterest (26.6%).[5]

In fact, we know that 25% of those aged 13–17 left Facebook in 2014 and went to Snapchat, Whisper, and Secret.[5]

If we only had to worry about these platforms, it wouldn't seem as overwhelming. Unfortunately, here are ten more possible social media platforms your daughter might be on (in no particular order):

> Yik Yak
> Whisper
> Secret

Wut
Rumr
Finsta (Fake Instagram Account)
Tumblr
Kik
WhatsApp
Tinder

Many of these may be obsolete by the time you read this book because app developers are continually creating more and more apps they hope will appeal to teenagers' minds.

Now that you are a near-expert on social media platforms for tween and teenaged girls (just kidding), you are almost ready for The Live Shoot! But before we go on, let's go behind the scenes and find out all of the details for this week's Episode.

Behind the Scenes Setup (for Dad)

Set Location
Choose your favorite place to get waffles. Make sure it has free Wi-Fi and remember to choose a table or stool in a somewhat private spot where you and your daughter can talk openly.

3-2-1 Action! Activity Overview
The main idea of today's 3-2-1 Action! Activity is to co-write a set of Social Media Guardrails to help your daughter set boundaries on what she posts and doesn't post on her favorite social media apps.

Stage Checklist

- Confirm your waffle and Wi-Fi location

- Plan on this Episode taking an hour to an hour and a half

- Invite your daughter and book it on your calendar (have her bring her smartphone if she has one)

- Your laptop and/or smartphone

- *Friday Night Lights for Fathers and Daughters* Book

- Social Media Guardrails Template: MarkLaMaster. com/smguardrails

- Some paper and a pen or pencil for each of you

🎥 The Live Shoot!

Today is the day you and your daughter will be shooting the Waffles and Wi-Fi Episode! You have chosen your favorite place to get waffles, have reviewed The Pitch, The SCRIPT"-ure, and have prayed about this precious time with your daughter.

Pre-Episode Prayer

Heavenly Father,

As _____ (daughter's name) and I explore and discuss social media today, please guide our conversation so that all we do glorifies You. Help us to trust Your Word as the ultimate authority on what we share with the world on social media. If _____ (daughter's name) meets resistance with what she may have already shared online, allow her the courage to reveal her secrets and know that she is covered by Your grace and Your forgiveness. Lord, please provide me with the knowledge and wisdom on how to best communicate with _____ (daughter's name) and help her to trust that I care about her safety online and beyond.

In Jesus' name we pray,
Amen.

3, 2, 1, Action! Activity

And . . . ACTION! Today's Episode is already off to a great start. Your daughter knows the Episode title, the "SCRIPT"-ure, and is excited to order her favorite waffle creation—whip cream is required!

After you each get comfortable and settled in your little corner of the world, go ahead and get right to it. If your daughter already has a smart phone or is active on social media, ask her the five questions below. If your daughter does not have a smart phone and is not on social media, skip to the "SCRIPT"-ure section that follows.

1. What social media apps do you use on a daily basis? Can you show me on your phone?

You may get a variety of answers, such as, "It's kind of personal dad," "You know, Snapchat, Instagram, and stuff like that," or "I don't have any."

2. If you could take a wild guess, how many times do you check your phone per day?

3. How does it feel to get a message, a "like," a "snap," a "follower," or a "friend" on one of the apps?

4. Would you be willing to explain your answers a bit more and give me a few examples? Could you show me an example on your phone?

5. Have you ever felt mad, angry, hurt, or upset after receiving a message of any kind? Can you tell me more about it? Did you respond to the post or just ignore it?

At this time, take a few minutes to read through Kelly's story from The Pitch. As you read aloud, notice how your daughter is reacting. Is she engaged, nervous, or anxious? Then ask her:

6. Have you ever been asked to send naked pictures of yourself? If you have, have you ever sent them?

I know this might be extremely awkward for both of you. But, you *have* to ask the tough questions to get to know your daughter. She may not show it right now, but she appreciates you asking her these types of questions.

If your daughter answers "Yes" to sending nude pictures of herself, I would encourage you to put this book away and forego the rest of the Episode for a later time, and focus only on this subject. I would also encourage you to involve your wife or your daughter's mother as soon as possible, with your daughter's permission. You may even consider seeking professional help for your daughter.

If your daughter answers "Yes" to the question about the request for nude pictures of herself, but "No" to taking pictures of herself and sending them, ask her how the request made her feel.

Follow up this question with: *Did you ever tell anyone about it?*

If your daughter answered "No" to both the questions in #6 above, and it is evident that this topic is embarrassing and disgusting to her, make sure to review the recent research from Nancy Jo Sales, Peggy Orenstein, and Jesse Weinberger in The Pitch.

No matter which way your daughter answered, make sure to share the following statistic with your daughter: Up to 48% of girls have received a sext message and, on average, sexting begins in 5th grade![2,3]

Above all else, remind your daughter that she is loved by God and by you and that she is forgiven—God makes bad things turn good.

"SCRIPT"-ture

Next, ask your daughter to read today's "SCRIPT"-ure aloud:

To act justly and to love mercy and to walk humbly with your God.

Micah 6:8

After reading Micah 6:8, share this simple but powerful social media filter with your daughter.

1. Is what you are about to say worth contributing to the conversation? Will it help you to tell your story?

2. If I went back and read all of my [social media] statuses [posts], would I recognize me?

3. If I went back and read all of my [social media] statuses [posts], would I know that I was a Christian?[6]

4. Hannah asked me to add this question: Will your post or text glorify God?

I found this simple, but effective filter during my research while reading, *Enough: 10 Things We Should Tell Our Teenage Girls*, by Kate Conner. Conner's writing makes for an easy read and is packed full of amazing parenting nuggets. I had Hannah read Conner's book for girls, titled, *10 Things for Teen Girls*, which is essentially a companion book to *Enough*, but written to girls rather than parents. Conner is unapologetic in her Christian views but has a way of convicting the reader to respond with love.

You and your daughter have covered some pretty deep material. You have asked some extremely personal questions and have discussed a simple filter for your daughter to use as she responds to her social media posts.

Social Media Guardrails

Now it's time to take all that you have learned and co-write your Social Media Guardrails. Why guardrails and not guidelines? Well, just take a quick peek at their respective definitions. A guideline is defined as "a general rule, principle, or piece of advice." (Dictionary.com) When I think of guideline, I think of all of the guidelines at our work places . . . boring! Guidelines are often overlooked and seem to hide in the fine print.

Guardrails, on the other hand, help establish a strong visual element that helps protect us from danger. Here are my favorite definitions of a guardrail: "a barrier placed along the edge of a dangerous place," (Merriam-Webster Dictionary) and a "protective railing." (Dictionary.com)

From one dad to another, I would encourage you to delay social media access for your daughter as long as possible. Legally, she must be 13 years old to have her own account anyway. Yes, social media is becoming more and more a part of the genetic makeup of our digital world. The more we educate her about texting and social media, the better she will be prepared to make her decision when you approve.

The Social Media Guardrails that you will co-write with your daughter will allow you to help protect her from the dangers of social media and will show her your concern for her safety.

To begin co-writing your Social Media Guardrails, feel free to print off a copy of The Social Media Guardrails Template at MarkLaMaster.com/smguardrails or just use a piece of paper and start writing.

Here are a few topics that will get you started. Remember dad; these are guardrails only, not a restrictive list of "100 things your daughter cannot do on social media or else" list. I recommend a one-page set of guardrails that you can post in a well-traveled location in your home.

- Usage Time Limit
- Social Media Curfew (all devices)
- Consequences for dented or broken guardrails
- Purity Issues (Nude pictures, explicit language)
- Accountability (Internet filtering software)
- Friends and Followers
- Personal Filter (3 questions from Kate Conner and *Enough*)
- Accepted Social Media Sites vs. Not-Accepted Social Media Sites
- Consequences of not following the Guardrails

Limit your Guardrails to one page. Don't get too detailed. Make each Guiderail simple, and to the point so no one gets confused. We are not going for perfection here; we are going for protection.

Make sure both of you sign and date the Social Media Guardrails you co-write, and make sure you abide by them.

When you get home, make sure to display this somewhere that is visible to all members of the family—it will serve as a reminder to all of you and help keep you accountable to the Guardrails.

🎟 Backstage Pass

You and your daughter have covered some emotionally heavy topics and have co-written your own Social Media Guardrails. Now it's time to lighten things up a bit. Dads, remember that asking questions helps you to develop a deeper relationship with your daughter. Here are a few more questions to ask your daughter before the Red Carpet Interview.

1. Can you tell me what you were thinking when I read the story about Kelly and Jake?

2. What do you think about the consequences of not following the Social Media Guardrails that we wrote today? Do you feel that they are fair?

3. What do you feel is the worst thing that you have ever posted on social media?

4. Going forward, what will you change about your social media habits?

5. Does it help to consider your faith as a filter before you post to social media? Explain.

🎬 Red Carpet Interview

The red carpet has been laid out for you. Your smartphone camera is being pointed at you with your daughter behind the lens. She has a few questions for you:

Red Carpet Questions for Dad

1. Dad, what kind of waffles did you order today? How were they?

2. What is one thing that surprised you about how I use social media and why?

3. Dad, do the Social Media Guardrails that we wrote today apply to you?

4. What do you think social media will be like in the future?

Red Carpet Questions for Daughter

1. What waffles do you like the best? Why?

2. _____ (daughter's name), can you share your biggest "aha" moment about social media that you learned today?

3. What is your favorite social media app that you couldn't live without? Why?

4. Which of the Social Media Guardrails do you feel will be the most challenging to follow? Why?

5. How many popcorn buckets would you give today's Episode? (Circle your choice)

 **Hannah's Take**

I believe you can still stay connected to your friends without social media. Texting and calling works great, too! But, if you choose to use social media, there are a lot of opportunities to glorify God.

No matter what type of communication you use, ask

yourself if what you are posting honors and glorifies God. What God thinks of your post is more important than what others think!

—Hannah

Check out the *Friday Night Lights for Fathers Private Facebook Group* and see what other dads and daughters are talking about. Can anyone say extra whipped cream?

Episode 5
Dream and Do

Episode Guide

Theme
Calling and Career

"SCRIPT"-ure

> *For we are His workmanship, created in Christ Jesus for good works, which God prepared beforehand that we should walk in them.*
>
> *Ephesians 2:10 NKJV*

Set Location
Your home

3-2-1 Action! Activity
Time Capsule

The Pitch

Katherine Coleman was born on August 26, 1918, in the small town of White Sulphur Springs, West Virginia. She was the baby of the family, but that never seemed to stop her. Her dad, Joshua, was a jack-of-all trades working as a janitor at the Greenbrier Hotel. Katherine's mom, Joylette, was a teacher for some time until she began raising her family.

Joshua and Joylette recognized Katherine's intellectual gifts at a young age, especially her affinity for mathematics. Perhaps it was her love of counting that tipped them off. Reflecting on her early childhood, Katherine reminisced, "I counted everything. I counted the steps to the road, the steps up to church, the number of dishes and silverware I washed . . . anything that could be counted, I did."[1]

At the age of 10, Katherine completed 8th grade. Because the county lacked the proper education for her abilities, the family looked elsewhere. Her dad saw the potential in his daughter and made the decision to move his family 120 miles to Institute, West Virginia, so Katherine could receive a high school education.

Dads, we all want to do the best we can for our daughters, but would any of us move our family 120 miles to attend high school?

The high school education that Katherine received was actually on the campus grounds of West Virginia State University. Katherine continued to excel. During high school, Katherine was mentored by several teachers who encouraged her to pursue her love of math, especially geometry.

Katherine breezed through high school at age 13 and went straight on to college, graduating summa cum laude with degrees in Mathematics and French—at the age of 18! One of her professors even developed a course in analytical geometry specifically for Katherine.

Upon graduation, Katherine accepted a teaching position at a local school. But Katherine's education wasn't quite complete. After Katherine was married (now Katherine Johnson), she was handpicked to enroll in West Virginia University's graduate math program. Katherine decided not to complete the program because she wanted to start a family.

In a recent *Vanity Fair* article, Katherine shared one of her favorite sayings from her dad,

"You are as good as anybody in this town, but you're no better."[2]

A second dad lesson from Katherine's dad for those of us raising daughters—encourage them to do their best while teaching them humility.

Katherine enjoyed motherhood, but her love of mathematics was still simmering in her heart and soul. So, when a family member recommended she apply for a computing position at the National Advisory Committee for Aeronautics (NACA), Katherine complied. Within a year, Katherine was working with other women, calculating numbers for NACA's engineers.[1]

As you might imagine, Katherine rose through the ranks within NACA because of her mathematical abilities. But it wasn't her technical ability alone that promoted her—Katherine asked questions. "The women did what they were told to do," Katherine explained. "They didn't ask questions or take the task any further. I asked questions; I wanted to know why. They got used to me asking questions and being the only woman there."[1]

I can picture the Coleman's dinner table conversations where Katherine's parents are encouraging their 4 young children to ask "why"—not to be satisfied with just doing the work, but truly understanding it. As dads, we can instill this curiosity in our kids with a simple dinner time conversation and helping them envision their future careers.

Eventually, Katherine was again handpicked for a job that required an expert in analytical geometry, a course that her college professor designed just for her. She accepted the position and the rest is history.

By now, you may know that Katherine is Katherine Johnson, the NASA "computer" from the best-selling book by Margot Lee Shetterly, *Hidden Figures*. Katherine calculated the trajectory for the first American space flight of Alan Shepard in 1961 and was requested by John Glenn to confirm IBM computer calculations for his first orbital mission.

Here is how Shetterly summarizes Glenn's trust in Katherine:

Spaceship-flying computers might be the future, but it didn't mean John Glenn had to trust them. He did, however, trust the brainy fellas who controlled the computers. And the brainy fellas who controlled the computers trusted their computer, Katherine Johnson. It was as simple as eighth-grade math: by the transitive property of equality, therefore, John Glenn trusted Katherine Johnson.[2]

In fact, Glenn is quoted as saying, "Get the girl [Katherine Johnson] to check the numbers"—if she says the numbers are good, he was good to go.[2]

Other sources state that Glenn had asked for Katherine specifically and refused to fly unless she verified the calculations.[3]

In another recent interview, Katherine again references her father. She said he was "the tallest, straightest man in the area." She loved her father a great deal, and he was a big influence in her life, teaching her many things.[1]

Katherine's father is an example for all of us dads with daughters to follow. Do we walk "tall" and "straight" in all that we do?

Katherine retired from NASA in 1986 after 33 years of service. Her contributions to the space program were certainly immeasurable. However, as a black woman in a predominantly white male profession, her contributions to gender and racial equality far exceeded anything she could have ever dreamed of.

Katherine's story of hard work, perseverance, and passion for her lifelong career is a powerful and inspiring story for both dads and daughters and led me to ask myself how I am leading my daughter to pursue her gifts, talents, and passions.

I can't wait to get to the Behind the Scenes Setup for you, but I want to ask you a few questions about your daughter first:

- Do you know what your daughter's favorite subject in school is?

- Are you aware of how she is performing in school?

- Do you actively participate in helping her with her homework?

- Are you able to confidently list out her areas of giftedness?

- If someone asked you what your daughter dreams of becoming when she grows up, would you be able to respond correctly?

- Do you frequently acknowledge her for the things she does well in?

- Or, do you more often focus on the areas that she needs to improve?

The reason I ask is because I believe we all need to do a bit of self-reflection on how we currently engage with our daughters when it comes to school, sports, or other activities before we start shooting this Episode.

If you are like me, I have come to realize that I often criticize before I compliment. My non-verbal reactions reveal my initial emotions without even thinking about it. I want to help coach my daughter on the areas that she needs to further develop rather than applaud her for the hundred other things she is doing well. I can't help it; I innately want to fix the problem and make it better. I need to work on my patience and my tone and choose my words more wisely.

Am I the only dad that feels or reacts this way? Help me out here, guys!

After learning about Katherine's dad, Joshua, and how he moved 120 miles to improve education options for his daughter, it convicted me to learn more about my daughter's future desires and career dreams.

Behind the Scenes Setup (for Dad)

Set Location
For this Episode only, it will be most convenient to shoot the footage at home.

3-2-1 Action! Activity Overview
I am so excited about today's 3-2-1 Action! Activity. You and your daughter will be constructing a Father/Daughter Time Capsule—complete with handwritten letters to each other, photos, career goals and dreams, and other prized objects to pack away for future discovery.

Please plan some extra time for this Episode to ensure that you have time to gather and create the items included in the Stage Checklist below.

Stage Checklist

- Schedule The Live Shoot! with your daughter and put in in your calendar
- Ask her what she would like to order for takeout or delivery
- 42-oz. empty oatmeal container (time capsule)
- Printer with photo paper
- Glue
- Paper and pen
- 📷 Father/Daughter "Time Capsule 20" printable
- MarkLaMaster.com/timecapsule20

- 2-GB flash drive

- Colored pencils or markers

- Handwritten letter to your daughter

  - Dad, the purpose of this letter is to tell your daughter how much you love her, how proud of her you are, that you believe in her, and that you will always be there for her as long as you are able. Make sure it is handwritten, not typed. Trust me.

The Live Shoot!

The day for the *Dream and Do* Episode is at hand. You have gathered as many of the materials in the Stage Checklist as possible, have written your letter to your daughter, and have your 2-GB flash drive.

Before you get to the shoot, take a minute and pray the prayer below with your daughter.

Pre-Episode Prayer

Heavenly Father,

Only You know our future plans (Jeremiah 29:11). Please help _____ (daughter's name) and me trust in the plans that You have already prepared for us. As _____'s (daughter's name) dad, I pray for Your guidance as I help raise her and lead her to the calling You have established for her. You have blessed _____ (daughter's name) with so many gifts, and I pray that You reveal how she can best use her gifts to glorify You in her life and in her career. As her Dad, I pray for patience as You provide insight and inspiration as

_____ (daughter's name) prepares for a career that always points to You.

In Jesus' name we pray,
Amen

After praying, have your daughter read today's "SCRIPT"-ture aloud. Let it soak in for a minute and refer back to it occasionally as you work on the 3-2-1 Action! Activity.

> *For we are His workmanship, created in Christ Jesus for good works, which God prepared beforehand that we should walk in them.*
>
> *Ephesians 2:10 NKJV*

3-2-1 Action! Activity

First things first—food! Because you will be hanging out at home, make sure you grab some takeout and have it ready to go.

Your daughter may or may not like doing crafts, but once you explain that you are making a Father/Daughter Time Capsule together, she will love it.

You don't need to go through all of the details yet, but let your daughter know that you want to help her realize her goals, her dreams, and will do all that you can to help her with her future career.

Then, ask her the following questions: (Make sure to write her answers down on this page.)

1. How are things going at school?

2. What is your favorite subject? Why?

3. Do I help you enough with your homework or would you like more help?

4. What would you say that God has gifted you with? OR What subjects or sports seem to be easy for you?

5. What do you dream of becoming after high school?

6. Do I recognize you enough for the things you do well?

7. Or, do I focus more on the things that I think you need to improve on?

I know, what does this have to do with making a time capsule? Well, the National Center for Fathering conducted a survey of teenage girls who attended their Father/Daughter program. Each girl was asked this question: "What are two questions your dad could ask you to demonstrate that he really cares about what's going on in your life?"

The results may surprise you, especially if your daughter doesn't show any interest in answering any of the questions you ask her.

1. Daughters desired a daily review. They wanted to be asked questions like: "What happened at school today?" "How's it going?" "Did everything go well with your friends today?" "Did any bad things happen today?" Daughters feel cared for when their dads make an effort to connect to their everyday world.

2. Daughters hoped their dads would ask questions which had emotional implications. These included questions like: "Do you know how much I love you?" "How are you doing lately as far as emotional stuff?" "Are you upset about anything?" "How are you feeling?"

3. Daughters wanted their dads to ask questions related to **their future and their faith**. Daughters wanted

their dads to ask them: "What are your goals?" "What are you thinking about your future?" "What is God showing you?" "How is your spiritual life, your quiet times and your relationship with God?" One girl commented, "I like it when my dad digs deep and asks me specific questions about faith and my future."[5]

Whether they show it or not, our daughters crave questions from us. I don't know about you, but this motivates and inspires me to connect even more with my daughter. I hope it does for you, too.

All right, I know you and your daughter are champing at the bit to tackle this whole time capsule project. Go ahead and get started.

It's time to engage your creative side. Feel free to decorate the time capsule as you like. Odds are you or your daughter has been gifted with a tiny bit of artistic ability.

But, if you are like me, I want something I can print off and move on to the next step. If this is you, no worries, I had a Father/Daughter Time Capsule Cover printable created for you. You can find it at MarkLaMaster.com/timecapsulecover. Just print it, and glue it onto the oatmeal container.

Next, each of you will fill out your own "Time Capsule 20" questionnaire. (If you haven't printed it yet, you can do so now by clicking here: MarkLaMaster.com/timecapsule20)

It will only take her a couple of minutes. While you are both filling out the questionnaire, you can sneak your handwritten letter to your daughter into the container. If she sees you doing it, no big deal—tell her she can't read it until you open the time capsule.

After she is done with the "Time Capsule 20" questionnaire, take a selfie of the two of you, send it to your printer, and add the photo to your time capsule.

Then, dads, it's up to you and your daughter as to what items to add to your time capsule. Here is a list of some cool ideas that you may want to add:

- A copy of your local or national newspaper
- Your "My One Word" or favorite Bible verse
- Favorite magazine
- Favorite childhood toy
- An old smartphone
- Favorite clothing catalog
- Favorite soda can or snack package
- Pictures of:
  - Your daughter's room
  - Your family
  - Your pet(s)
  - Your family
  - Your friends
  - Gas prices
- Video clips of: (saved on the 2-GB flash drive)
  - Your Red Carpet Interview, of course
  - A tour of your home
  - Your favorite places
  - You reading your "Time Capsule 20" questionnaire

These are just a few ideas of what to include in your Father/Daughter Time Capsule. Feel free to add your own items or check out TimeCapsule.com or Pinterest (yes, I am recommending Pinterest!) for tons more time capsule ideas.

 Backstage Pass

Before rolling out the red carpet, take a moment to ask your daughter the following questions backstage:

- What worries you most about your future?

- What was your first memory of what you wanted to be when you grew up?

- Why do you think that has/has not changed? Explain.

- Do you trust that your faith in God will help lead you to your calling, your dreams, and your career?

Once you have asked the questions, decide:

- Where you want to place your time capsule.

  - Will you be burying it in your yard? Lock it in a safe deposit box at your bank? Be creative!

- When you will open your time capsule.

  - Your daughter's _____ (birthday). Near your daughter's college graduation? In 5, 10, or 15 years?

- How you will celebrate the opening of your time capsule.

Now, go put your Time Capsule in its designated place so it can wait to be opened on your agreed upon date in the future.

🎟 Red Carpet Interview

Red Carpet Questions for Dad

1. Dad, when you were my age, what did you want to be when you grew up? Why?

2. Who helped you reach your dream of becoming what you are today?

3. Did you become something completely different than you dreamed you would become?

4. Do you feel that you are using the gifts and talents God blessed you with and that you continue to seek His calling in your life?

Red Carpet Questions for Daughter

1. What do you think you will be doing and where do you think you will be living when we open our time capsule?

2. When you were my age, did you ever make a time capsule? If so, what did you put in it?

3. What is your favorite item that we put in the time capsule? Why?

4. Can you tell me about which one of the "Time Capsule 20" questions that you were most surprised about and why?

5. How many popcorn buckets would you give today's Episode? (Circle your choice)

🎬 Hannah's Take

If you're like me, you probably don't know what you want to be when you grow up. I know that I love animals, math, and piano, but have no idea how I could make a career out of them.

What I am continuing to understand, though, is that God already has a plan for me and for you! I want to encourage you to trust in Him to help guide you to serve Him in all that you do, not just in your career. I have recently started to pray about His plan for my future career. We all need to completely trust his perfect plan for our lives!

—Hannah

You can learn more about prayer in Episode 9!

Please share your time capsule creations in the *Friday Night Lights for Fathers Private Facebook Group.*

 **Episode 6** Date: ____ / ____ / _____

"Grattitude"

 ## Episode Guide

Theme
Gratitude and Contentment

"SCRIPT"-ure

> *The Lord is my shepherd. I shall not want.*
> *Psalm 23:1*

Set Location
Local Homeless Shelter

3-2-1 Action! Activity
Serve dinner at a local homeless shelter

 ## The Pitch

Despite living in the world's wealthiest nation, the 8th country in gross national income, and the 3rd country in annual salaries, we never seem to have enough.[1,2,3] We constantly, either consciously or unconsciously, compare ourselves to others.

Just a few days ago, I was feeling envious of a young friend of mine who is building a house that is nearly twice the square footage of our home, complete with a man cave, three-car garage, and sprinkler system. Never mind that our detached garage with a cement floor would be considered a luxury by the majority of families in the world.

As we dig into this Episode on "Grattitude," I want to share a few thoughts on an epidemic that has been emerging in the Western world over the past few decades. No, it's not measles, chicken pox, or ebola. In fact, the Centers for Disease Control and Prevention (CDC) neither tracks this epidemic nor has a cure for it. You see, the epidemic I am talking about is an epidemic of the heart—the "entitlement epidemic."

In their book, *The Entitlement Trap*, Richard and Eyre get right to the core of the entitlement epidemic. They describe entitlement as: ". . . an attitude of children who think they can have, should have, and deserve whatever they want, whatever their friends have—and that they should have it now, and not have to earn it or give anything up for it."[4]

The Merriam-Webster's definition of entitlement reads, "the belief that one is deserving or entitled to certain privileges."

I admit it, I often resort to a sense of entitlement and know that my entire family has been affected by the epidemic. We are certainly not cured of it, but we are certainly more conscious of it. Will we ever be cured of it? I don't know. What I do know is that the only way we began to chip away at this disease is to have a change of heart, to change our behaviors, and to look to Christ for direction.

Our role as the dad is extremely important as it pertains to the entitlement epidemic. If we have a heart full of entitlement, how can our kids not?

If we are to rid our hearts of entitlement and cure this widespread epidemic, where can we find the life-saving vaccine that we can inject into our own hearts and the hearts of our children?

In her book, *Raising Grateful Kids in an Entitled World*, Kristen Welch, one of my favorite parenting authors, has found the cure:

> *"When entitlement's poison begins to infect our hearts, gratitude is the antidote."*[5]

Gratitude? Seriously? With all of the advances in medicine, pharmacology, and surgery, the cure for the contentment-crusher, entitlement, is gratitude?

Does it come in a vial? A pill? As a nurse for nearly 20 years, believe me, most patients want the quick fix of a medicine they can pick up at their corner pharmacy, rather than hear the words, "you need to exercise, change your diet, and lose a few pounds."

The cure for entitlement takes time. It isn't cured overnight. It is a learned behavior.

The good news is we can help cure ourselves of entitlement as we help cure our daughters.

Before we get to the good stuff, is it all right if I share another story with you? To make it a bit more fun, I want to make it a bit of a competition. I have included a few quotes and a few facts as a challenge to all of you to make an educated guess about who the following story is about.

Most dads that have read this chapter are truly surprised by the person that I will reveal in a few moments.

"In spite of everything I still believe that people are really good at heart."[6]

"There's only one rule you need to remember: laugh at everything and forget everybody else! It sounds egotistical, but it's actually the only cure for those suffering from self-pity."[6]

Any guesses yet? If you get this correct at this point, you will be in the top 1%!

Here are a couple more quotes:

"As long as this exists, this sunshine and this cloudless sky, and as long as I can enjoy it, how can I be sad?"[6]

"Riches, prestige, everything can be lost. But the happiness in your heart can only be dimmed; it will always be there as long as you live, to make you happy again.

Whenever you're feeling lonely or sad, try going to the loft on a beautiful day and looking outside. Not at the houses and the rooftops, but at the sky. As long as you can look fearlessly at the sky, you'll know that your pure within and will find happiness once more."[6]

The person who spoke these wise words of wisdom lived in a home that was around 500 square feet. Compare that to the average size of a single-family home in 2016—a whopping 2,687 square feet![7]

The quotes are from a book that has sold more than 30 million copies in over 67 different languages since its first printing.

The author never knew it was printed.

Any guesses now? Most likely you have either read the book or have at least heard about it.

Before I reveal this insightful author's name, I want to share a few excerpts from *The Traveler's Gift*, by Andy Andrews. Andrews, one of the most gifted storytellers of our time, shared this author's story and used it to illustrate one of his "Seven Decisions That Determine Personal Success."

She was thin and sharply featured with dark and wavy hair and eyes so black that they shined. She appeared to be perhaps twelve or thirteen and wore a faded blue cotton dress that seemed at home in the dingy room.[8]

In response to a question about her living conditions shared with seven others, she responded:

Rough conditions? Yes, an ungrateful person might see this place as too small for eight people, a diet that is limited and has portions that are too meager, or only three dresses for two girls to share. But gratefulness is a choice. I see an annex that hides eight people while others are being herded into railway cars. I see food that is generously provided by Miep, whose family uses their ration cards for us. I see an extra dress for my sister and me while there are surely others who have nothing. I choose to be grateful. I choose not to complain. [8]

When asked if she was always in a good mood, this brave young woman answered:

Of course, not . . . But if I ever find myself in a bad mood, I immediately make a choice to be happy. In fact, it is the first choice I make every day. I say out loud to my mirror, 'Today, I will choose to be happy!' [8]

Lastly, Andy Andrews writes the following summary from our unknown author:

My God has bestowed upon me many gifts, and for those I will always be grateful . . . I do not wish to be seen as a greedy child, unappreciative and disrespectful. I am grateful for sight and sound and breath. If ever in my life there is a pouring out of blessings beyond that, then I will be grateful for the miracle of abundance . . . I am the possessor of a grateful spirit . . . Today I will choose to be happy. [8]

Dads, these words were written by a young woman, most likely similar in age to your own daughter right now. Her name—Anne Frank. Yes, wisdom way beyond her 14 years. She purposely chose to be grateful despite living conditions that most of us would have cowered in. Anne Frank chose not to complain about what she didn't have and instead chose to be happy for all that God had given her.

Can you imagine a world full of young women like Anne

Frank? A world where our daughters were grateful for what they have rather than feeling entitled to have it all—the latest iPhone, lululemon yoga pants, or a Snapchat account?

I can, and I believe that you can, too. I also believe we dads can help our daughters pursue a happy heart and a grateful attitude—a term I have named "Grattitude"—a *grat*eful at*titude.* "Grattitude" may just cure the entitlement epidemic that has poisoned all of our hearts with materialism, wanting more, and expecting everything our friends have.

It all starts with leading our daughters to make a simple decision—the decision to be happy with what they already have.

 Behind the Scenes Setup (for Dad)

Set Location
Local Homeless Shelter or Food Shelf

3-2-1 Action! Activity Overview
"Grattitude" is the state of pursuing happiness through a grateful attitude. As Kristen Welch so eloquently explains, "When entitlement's poison begins to infect our hearts, gratitude is the antidote." The main lesson in today's Episode is to help lead our daughters to "Grattitude" and crush the entitlement epidemic.

Serving others less fortunate than we are is one of the best ways to help our daughters really understand how much they truly have. Let's be honest, we often take the food we have for granted. Whether it is a home-cooked meal, a fast food combo, or a sit-down meal at our favorite restaurants, most of us have easy access to food. Most of us have never experienced true hunger.

Serving food at a homeless shelter or food shelf will help open our daughters' eyes to the real-life, day-to-day challenges that many families in our communities' experience.

Food is not a commodity, an afterthought, or a simple task for many families. Food is the priority for daily existence. It is what many people wake up thinking about and go to bed worrying about.

Stage Checklist

- Invite your daughter to help you schedule a volunteer opportunity at your local homeless shelter or food shelf.

- Contact your local homeless shelter or food shelf and schedule a time to serve a meal. (If you are unsure about how to locate a homeless shelter or food shelf, just Google "homeless shelter" or "food shelf near me.")

- Put the date and time on your calendar.

- Review The Pitch section of this Episode and memorize the "SCRIPT"-ure: *The Lord is my shepherd. I shall not want. Psalm 23:1*

- Confirm the materials and/or groceries that your local homeless shelter or food shelf requests of you.

🎥 The Live Shoot!

Ensure that you have enough time to travel to the homeless shelter or food shelf that you will be serving. Double-check that you have all of the items you were requested to bring with you. As you hop into the car, take a moment to tell your daughter how much you love her. Tell her that you are so proud of her for her serving heart. Then pray with her before you put your vehicle in drive.

Pre-Episode Prayer

Heavenly Father,

We know that you came to serve, not to be served (Matthew 20:28). As we serve those less fortunate than us today, please help us to be more like You. Help _____ (daughter's name) and me rid our minds of the entitlement that we so often struggle with. Instead, help us to fill our hearts with happiness and gratefulness for what you have already given us. As we serve others today, may Your light shine through us so others can see Your glory. We pray that today we better understand the words of Your mighty servant David, "The Lord is my shepherd. I shall not want" (Psalm 23:1). Help _____ (daughter's name) and me to crave contentment rather than embrace the entitlement that is so prevalent in this world.

In Jesus' name we pray,
Amen

3-2-1 Action! Activity
As you are driving to the homeless shelter or food shelf, ask your daughter if she has heard of Anne Frank or has read her diary. Either way, summarize, in your own words, how she chose to be happy, not to complain, and chose to be grateful for all that God had blessed her with.

Ask your daughter if she knows what entitlement means—(reminder: entitlement is an attitude of children who think they can have, should have, and deserve whatever they want, whatever their friends have—and that they should have it now, and not have to earn it or give anything up for it).

Then, ask your daughter if she believes that she feels entitled to anything. Whether she believes she feels entitled or not, share something you have felt entitled to.

Before you enter into the homeless shelter or food shelf, give your daughter the following advice:

- Many of the people you serve tonight may be a bit embarrassed to be here today.

- Look everyone in the eye.

- Don't judge the people. Each person has a unique story as to why they have to be walking through the food line today.

- They wouldn't be there if they didn't have to be.

- Serve them with a joyful heart.

- Think of 5 things you are grateful for as you serve tonight.

- Think of 5 things you could live without as you serve tonight.

As you walk into the building, ask God to give you a servant's heart. As my mentor and coach, Kary Oberbrunner, says, "Show up, filled up!" Then, get to it!

🎫 Backstage Pass

Once you have completed serving (and cleaning up), head to a location that you and your daughter can talk in private and film your Red Carpet Interview. This may be at the homeless shelter or the food shelf, or it may be at your favorite place to get a quick snack. No matter the location, just don't go home quite yet. If you and your daughter are anything like Hannah and me, once we enter our house, we seem to find way too many distractions and never complete the Episode.

Now that you are Backstage, ask your daughter the following questions:

1. What emotions are you feeling right now?

2. What 5 things did you think of that you are grateful for?

3. What 5 things did you think of that you could live without?

4. Did anything make you uncomfortable while serving today?

5. What surprised you most about serving today?

6. How do you think you would feel if our family had to go to a homeless shelter or a food shelf?

7. Do you have a different impression of the homeless after serving tonight?

8. Look up the following website: globalrichlist.com Then, ask your daughter: Do you realize how fortunate we are? Tell her your combined family income and have her it enter it on the website.

Both of you will soon find out how fortunate you and your family are compared to the rest of the world!

🎬 Red Carpet Interview

Red Carpet Questions for Dad

1. Dad, have you ever served at a homeless shelter or food shelf before? Can you tell me a bit about why or why not?

2. What did you learn about me as a person today?

3. Have you ever struggled with having enough money to buy food? Have you ever known anyone who has

had to go to a homeless shelter or food shelf? Can you tell me a bit about it?

4. Have you ever felt entitled to anything? I would love to hear more about it!

Red Carpet Questions for Daughter

1. Where did we serve today and what did we do?

2. What was the most rewarding part of serving those in need today?

3. What one thing will you never forget about today's Episode?

4. After today's Episode, do you have a better understanding of what entitlement means? Explain.

5. Now that you better understand what entitlement is, what have or do you still feel entitled to? Can you tell me a bit more about it?

6. How many popcorn buckets would you give today's Episode? (Circle your choice)

 **Hannah's Take**

Being content can be really hard, especially for a teenage girl! I have really struggled with comparing myself to others and wanting what they have, not even thinking about all that God has given me.

When you begin to realize that you are getting caught up in the worldly ways of entitlement and jealousy, ask God to get your mind focused on Him. Ask Him to open your eyes to see all of the blessings He has given you. I thank God for the things that I take for granted, for family, and for anything else I can think of.

The most important thing by far is to thank God for all that He is and all that He does. No matter how bad your circumstances are, you can always be thankful for God. Our ultimate goal is to be content in Christ alone, meaning that if we had nothing else, God would be all we needed. We can only get to that point with God!

—Hannah

Let's hear those "Grattitude" stories inside the *Friday Night Lights for Fathers Private Facebook Group*. Any Red Carpet Interview "A-ha moments?"

Episode 7
Weight or Wait?

Date: _____ / _____ / _____

Episode Guide

Theme
Boys and Boundaries

"SCRIPT"-ure

> *"So again, I say, a man must love his wife as a part of himself; and the wife must see to it that she deeply respects her husband—obeying, praising, and honoring him."*
>
> *Ephesians 5:33 TLB*

Set Location
Local Park, Neighborhood, or Your Own Backyard

3-2-1 Action! Activity
Geocaching

The Pitch

Where do you want your daughters to get advice about understanding boys and what's going on inside their minds? *Teen Vogue? Seventeen? Girls' Life?*

I asked my wife where she went to for advice about boys and dating when she was a teenager. Without hesitation, she told me *Teen* and *Seventeen* magazines, followed by advice from her sister who happened to be five years older than her. Not her parents—definitely not her dad. Certainly, not the Bible.

According to the following statistics, it appears my wife wasn't the only teen seeking advice from magazines:

- *Teen Vogue* had 5.4 million unique visitors in 2016 and over 1 million print subscribers.[1]

- According to their website, "*Seventeen* is the largest monthly teen media brand, reaching more than 15 million readers in print and online every month."[2]

- *Girls' Life* boasts an average of 500,000 unique views per month and nearly 1.9 million readers.[3]

With just about 42 million teenage girls living in the U.S., my math reveals that about 22 million (just over 52%) teenage girls are reading at least one of these teen magazines.

You might be thinking—how can I help my daughter when it comes to understanding boys, and how can I guide her through this whole dating thing? First of all, you have instant credibility that no one else in your family possesses—you lived through it.

Dad, you can build on that credibility, especially with your daughter, and you have a unique opportunity to share your thoughts, your experience, and your wisdom about the teenage boys' perspective.

Knowing that it has been a few years since we were teenagers, I thought I would seek additional advice from some experts a bit closer to the situation. You have to admit that we might be a bit out-of-touch with the teenage culture—you know, the fact that we grew up pre-social media and pre-iPhone.

Instead of looking to the usual "experts" on this one, I decided to see if I could find a few of my own. Want to know who I found?

Here are a few clues:

- A 19-year-old entrepreneur with her own online magazine

- A Harvard graduate and former Wall Street executive
- A former juvie turned youth relationship expert

Any ideas? Read on and check out what I found.

Let's start with the 19-year-old entrepreneur with her own online magazine. I ran across her work about a year ago when I started researching this book. I knew when I read her work that I wanted to share it with you.

Livy Jarmusch, now 22, grew up in a loving Christian family. With her passion for writing, Livy decided to start her own online magazine for young women, CrownofBeautyMagazine.com.

Since then, she has written several books and serves countless young women as they navigate through their teenage years and beyond.

In her knowledge-packed eBook, *When Life Feels Like a Taylor Swift Song: A Girl's Guide to Boys*, Jarmusch openly admits that she did not date in middle school or high school. Instead of giving advice on teenage dating, she gives girls the following advice:

> Being friends with a boy is ten-trillion times smarter than diving head first into a "boyfriend-girlfriend" relationship. So many girls make the mistake of hopping from boyfriend to boyfriend and can never stay in a longer-term relationship. Why? Because they have not learned how to simply . . . be friends with a boy![4]

Instead of making the dive into dating, Jarmusch challenges the so-called teen magazine "experts" by making this statement: "A girl must first learn how to be a fantastic friend, and be confident in herself before she can be a great girlfriend."[4]

This might sound a bit odd, but despite my hours and hours of researching, reading, and recollecting, it took a 19-year-old woman to reveal the true secret of what guys are really seeking from the opposite sex: respect. "Guys look to the girls they know for respect and affirmation."[4]

Dads, from a guys' perspective, didn't Jarmusch nail it? We seek respect for all that we do, all that we are, and all that we want to become. So, instead of pushing our daughters into the dating world, why not empower them to encourage their male peers to become the best version of themselves.

On my quest to figure out how to help our daughters better understand the teenage boy's mind, I read this statement by a Harvard graduate and former Wall Street executive, Shaunti Feldhahn: "While it may seem odd to most of us, the male need for respect and affirmation—especially from the main girl in his life—is even more important than love."[5]

Feldhahn also added, "...what men need is unconditional respect—to be respected for who they are, apart from how they do."[5] I agree, but found this next statement to clearly explain what I want to teach my daughter: "If you, as a young woman, learn how to treat guys with respect right now, these attitudes and habits will carry over into your marriage one day."[5]

And now, folks, is the perfect time to seek wisdom from God's Word.

Ephesians 5, which is often referred to as the marriage passage in the Bible. But ironically, it never advises wives to "love" their husbands, rather, wives are told to treat their husbands with *respect*.[5]

> "So again, I say, a man must love his wife as a part of himself; and the wife must see to it that she deeply respects her husband—obeying, praising, and honoring him."
>
> Ephesians 5:33 (TLB)

But, your daughter might ask you in argument, "Why do all boys check out girls, especially the ones in skimpy outfits? Shouldn't they respect us as well?"

Feldhahn gives us the following advice: "We need to say right up front that we are not excusing wrong choices. But we all face temptations, and this is one of the main ones for guys."[5]

In their book, *For Young Women Only: What You Need to Know About How Guys Think*, Shaunti Feldhahn and her co-author, Lisa Rice, reveal the results of their study from over 400 guys between the ages of 15–20.

Here is the survey question:

Imagine you are sitting in class, and a new girl with a great body sits down a few desks over from you. What is your reaction to her?[5]

Any guesses on how what percentage of the guys said, "Nothing happens. It wouldn't affect me."

How about the "can't not be attracted to her" category?

Well, only 4% of the guys checked the "Nothing happens. It wouldn't affect me" box. The "can't not be attracted to her" category was checked by the other 96% of the guys![5]

Dads, we need to let our daughters know that the majority of guys will look, that yes, we are visual creatures, but that it doesn't mean that all guys are creepy. Rather, explain it this way, "Guys are designed by God to be attracted to both inner and outer beauty."[5]

We are now definitely getting inside of the teenage boy's mind. As we discuss boys and dating with our daughters, we must emphasize that the point of this new information is not to change how the guys in their lives behave, but to have a better understanding of their male peers' perspective.

Our next expert admits he was a juvie in high school, caught up in drugs, alcohol, and bad decisions. It was while he was in his padded cell that he realized his true purpose in life. Chad Eastham is now a sought-after speaker and has authored several books, including, *The Truth About Guys*.

The truth about guys from a guy's perspective—just what I was looking for to help us help our daughters better understand guys. As I began reading the book, I couldn't put it down. I was highlighting almost every page . . . then I read this:

> The two key ingredients that guys are looking for, more than anything else, are intelligence and kindness. Which ranks higher? Kindness. Guys like girls who are kind. The words sexy, sassy, athletic, tall, short, fashionable, funny, sexual, or hot are not what guys really want. If you're putting these words first in your life . . . you'll miss something. You'll miss being what we want—a kind, thoughtful, and compassionate person. When you go fishing for guys, kindness is the best bait you can put on your hook.[6]

We need to help our daughters dispel the myths they hear from the media and replace it with the truth: The good guys don't like mean girls. The good guys don't like girls that disrespect them. The good guys don't like girls that are self-centered and conceited.

Check this out! Eastham shares another golden nugget we can share with our daughters:

> Give it some thought. If you didn't look at the opposite sex through the lens of romance and love first but started looking at guys through the lens of friendship and care, perhaps all of your relationships would be stronger once they developed. I can't predict your future, but I think you'd wind up smiling a lot more![6]

BOOM!

I hope these three "experts" have helped you gain a new perspective into the minds of today's teenage male, but before we head any further with today's Episode, I am convicted to cover teenage dating. Please know that I realize the decision to allow your daughter to date is delicate and will take time, prayer, and much discussion.

Most important of all, our daughters must understand that they should respect the guys in their life, but that the guys must respect them as well. We must instill this important message in our daughters' minds. One way to do this is to have a conversation about boundaries with boys.

As Hannah approached her teenage years, we were led to provide Hannah with some boundaries for dating. Both of us were relatively new to this whole dating thing and felt fortunate that Hannah hadn't yet entered the "boy crazy" stage of adolescence.

Despite both Jen and me dating in middle school, we wanted our kids to wait a bit longer. In our house, neither Hannah or Lincoln is allowed to go on one-on-one dates until they are at least 16 years old.

Why? You might ask.

We became informed. We sought out wisdom. We prayed. We discussed the pros and cons. We asked God for guidance. We made this decision several years ago and provided our kids with our expectations, guidelines, and boundaries for dating.

Well, I couldn't help but realize that each of the three "experts" on the minds of teenage boys also discussed the topic of dating. Each expert discussed boundaries for dating. I couldn't believe it.

Here's what our three experts had to say about encouraging our daughters to set boundaries when and if you allow your daughter to date:

Livy Jarmusch:
"There is nothing wrong with setting boundaries. In fact, there is something wrong if you're not setting boundaries."[4]

Shaunti Feldhahn:
"Set boundaries! Almost every guy who felt some responsibility not to go "too far" believed it was critical to set boundaries."[5]

Chad Eastham:
"How do you know what your boundaries should be with someone you are dating? That's a great question. Don't do anything in private that you aren't okay doing in public. It keeps you from having to be sneaky, question your decisions, and defend the stuff you're doing. The second rule of thumb is to keep your bodies in an upright position when you are with each other. When the two of you decide to go horizontal, it becomes a microwave moment for guys. We go from zero to one hundred in a minute. Getting horizontal usually escalates and takes a couple further than they planned."[6]

Let me be clear, I am not telling you at what age you should allow your daughter to date, but I am encouraging you to help her set boundaries in her relationships.

I did a bit more digging about this whole dating thing because I want to give my daughter the best advice as she begins her "boy-crazy" phase, and I want to help you advise your daughter as well.

We all know what dating can lead to—yes, physical and emotional contact which may lead to sexual intercourse. I want to share with you some extremely shocking but convincing responses from teenage girls who ultimately decided to have sex as a teenager.

What I found out from young women who had decided, willingly or unwillingly, to "go all the way" and have sex while dating, before marriage, shocked me. Our next Episode, "A

Sticky Situation," will go into more detail about teenage sex, but I want to focus on the emotional aspects of sex while dating. It seems appropriate to mention the emotional impact teenage sex may cause during the dating Episode because, naturally, dating often leads to physical contact.

Despite the buildup and excitement of sex that our culture advertises to our teens, I want my daughter (and yours) to know what real-life teens feel after they have sex for the first time.

Jim Burns, author of *The Purity Code*, and Donna Freitas, author of *Sex and the Soul*, surveyed and interviewed teen girls from high school to college about how they felt after having sex for the first time.

Here is a sampling of words real-life teens are using to describe the emotions they feel after sex:

• Naughty	• Ashamed
• Guilt	• Alone
• Regret	• Disgusted
• Mistrust	• Duped
• Loss of Respect	• Abused
• Rejection	• Depression
• Sadness	• Anger
• Awkward	• Loneliness
• Used	• Frustration
• Dirty	• Fear
• Empty	• Worry[7, 8]

Let me ask you a question. Do you want your daughter carrying the weight of these emotions through her dating life as she begins her search for her soul mate, the one man that God has already chosen for her? The media will encourage her to have sex with a guy to make sure he is "the one," that they are compatible sexually, and that they can live together successfully.

Or, think about this—when your daughter is standing at the altar on her wedding day, would you rather that she was able to completely respect her husband and have her husband completely love her?

I believe all of us dads want our daughters to enter into marriage with as little emotional weight as possible. Sure, she will make some mistakes, but none of us would want her to be carrying the weight of regret, depression, sadness, emptiness, abuse, or shame, on her wedding day. Rather, we want to help our daughters' wedding day be filled with love, respect, friendship, integrity, and trust.

The weight of emotions caused by sexual sin is real, it is heavy, and it can have long-term consequences.

In contrast, love, respect, friendship, integrity, and trust are essentially weightless by comparison. If we can encourage our daughters to build friendships with guys, delay dating, and set boundaries on physical touch, we can help our daughters arrive at the altar on their wedding day as God planned it—even if they have already made bad decisions.

Behind the Scenes Setup (for Dad)

Set Location
Local Park or Your Neighborhood

3-2-1 Action! Activity Overview
The subject of boys and dating will be an ongoing discussion with your teenage daughter. So far, we have learned more about the minds of teenage boys and dating boundaries through experience, surveys, and observations from our

three experts. Using geocaching as your activity, your daughter will be on her way to making mature decisions about her relationships.

In order to help her envision her future wedding day, we will be using the homophones, weight and wait, to further illustrate emotional baggage or emotional freedom as it relates to our daughters' relationships.

Here's what you will need:

Stage Checklist

- Confirm the date and time of your geocache Episode and invite your daughter. Then, put it on the calendar.

- Determine the location for your geocache experience (local park, neighborhood, or your own backyard).

- You will need the following items:
  - A backpack your daughter can carry, and that can hold a bit of weight
  - Handheld GPS (Global Positioning Satellite) to pinpoint the exact location of your geocache
    - GPS options:
    - Smartphone GPS or Geocache apps (I used the geocaching.com free version)
    - If you want to step it up a notch and purchase a handheld GPS unit, I would recommend the Garmin eTrex GPS (about $100)
  - Five (5) bricks or larger rocks that you can write on and that will fit into your daughter's backpack

- Five (5) small, quarter-sized rocks that will fit into a small container (this will be the geocache that you hide)

    - I used rocks from my landscaping, but you can certainly buy "signing stones" at your local craft shop or even at Walmart.com

- A small container that will hold the 5, small quarter-sized rocks such as a small pouch or even a Ziploc bag

- A permanent marker

• Choose five (5) sinful emotions from the list below and write each one on separate bricks or larger rocks and then place them in your daughter's backpack:

- Naughty	- Ashamed
- Guilt	- Alone
- Regret	- Disgusted
- Mistrust	- Duped
- Loss of Respect	- Abused
- Rejection	- Depression
- Sadness	- Anger
- Awkward	- Loneliness
- Used	- Frustration
- Dirty	- Fear
- Empty	- Worry[7, 8]

• Next, choose five (5) emotions (make sure to choose **respect**) that you want your daughter to experience on her wedding day and write each one on separate small, quarter-sized rocks:

- Peaceful
- Content
- Loved
- Trust
- Thankfulness
- Secure
- Joy
- Faithful
- Goodness
- Appreciated
- **Respect**
- Valuable
- Confident
- Committed
- Safe
- Excitement

If you are a newbie geocacher (like me), I would recommend watching the brief Geocaching 101 video. You can also find this video on Geocaching.com. Once you have created your two sets of rocks and labeled them, place all of the bricks/rocks in the backpack for your daughter and set it aside.

- Place the small rocks with labels in the container (pouch or Ziploc) of your choice and think of where you want to hide your new geocache item for your daughter to find.

- Once you have decided where you want to hide your geocache (container or Ziploc with 5 small rocks), travel to the general location where you wish to hide it.

- Have your GPS/geocache app on your smartphone or your handheld GPS up and running.

- Make sure that your hiding spot is not within 0.1 mile of another geocache.

- For newbie geocachers ONLY: Watch the "Hiding Your First Geocache" video at geocaching.com/about/hiding.aspx

- Mark your waypoints, enter them into your geocache app, and send it in for review.

- Congrats! You did it! You hid your first ever geocache.

Well, that does it for Stage Checklist. I recommend gathering these items at least one day before you plan your Live Shoot!

The Live Shoot!

Dads, as you might imagine, the planning stage for this Episode is going to take a bit more time and creativity on your part.

I know of dads who have hidden their geocache (5 small rocks) at a park along a trail, in their neighborhood, or even their own backyard. Be creative with this Episode and have fun!

Pre-Episode Prayer

Heavenly Father,

Today, _____ (daughter's name) and I will be talking about a topic that may be uncomfortable and awkward at times. Please give me the courage to share this information with _____ (daughter's name), and help me to effectively communicate the lessons of today's Episode to her in a caring and compassionate way. Help us to better understand Your plan for dating relationships between boys and girls. May the boundaries that we discuss today help form a firm foundation in the life of _____'s (daughter's name) dating and romantic relationship.

In Jesus' name, we pray.
Amen

3-2-1 Action! Activity

All right geocache dads, let's get this Episode going. You have already done most of the leg work for this Episode— you have loaded your daughter's backpack, your geocache is hidden and marked, and you have learned a ton about the minds of teen guys, dating, and the emotions you want your daughter to have on her wedding day.

Once you and your daughter have arrived at your pre-determined Live Shooting! location, hand your daughter the backpack and let her know that you are going geocaching.

Share the title with her, "Weight or Wait." Explain that the topic of today's Episode is boys, dating, and boundaries.

During your hike/walk, I recommend that you take a break every five minutes and do the following:

Break 1

- Ask your daughter who she feels most comfortable talking to about guys and where she goes to get advice about boys.

  - Once she has answered, have her take a brick/ rock out of her backpack and have her read it aloud.

  - Take the brick/rock from her and let her know that this is one of the long-term, sinful emotions that physical relationships before marriage can cause.

Your daughter's backpack load is now a few pounds lighter. As you continue walking, ask your daughter about boy friends, boyfriends, or crushes she might have.

Break 2

- Ask her if she has any questions about guys—how they think, what they think, or how they act.

    - Make sure to share your own teenage experiences, and add some of our experts' advice on how and what boys are thinking. (e.g., I read in this book that three experts on teen relationships believe that being friends with boys before dating is the way to go). Feel free to use your own advice here as well.

    - Next, have her take out another brick/rock and have her read it to you. Explain that your hope and prayer for her is that she does not take this emotion into her marriage because of a decision she made while dating.

You are starting to break the ice here with your daughter. You are getting further along the trail. Don't be surprised if she starts asking you questions.

Break 3

- Ask your daughter if she has any questions for you about when you started dating. Be bold dads. If you want your daughter to open up to you, sharing your past is one great step forward.

    - Have her take out another brick/rock from her backpack. Once she reads it aloud, let her know that you will love her no matter what mistakes she makes in relationships, but that your goal as a dad is to help her make the best decisions.

As you continue, answer any questions your daughter might have. If she doesn't, appreciate the silence.

Break 4

- If your daughter hasn't started dating, ask her when she thinks it is appropriate to start dating.

- If your daughter has already started dating, ask her why she thinks dating at her age is beneficial. (Tough question, but give her some time to answer.)

  - When you have discussed the question, have her take out another brick/rock and read the word aloud.

  - If she hasn't dated, ask her if she feels dating and entering into a physical relationship with a guy is worth the potential of these emotions?

  - If she has dated, ask her if she has ever felt any of these emotions in her boyfriend relationships. Talk about it.

Things are getting pretty serious now, right? Keep pushing on; you are almost there!

Break 5

- Ask your daughter about the guy she would like to marry. What does he look like? What kind of personality does he have? Is he a Christian? Does he want to have children? What hobbies does he have? Why is he 'the one?'

- Now, have her take out the final brick/rock and read it. Then, have her pick up the backpack and ask her what it feels like.

  - Tell her that no matter what kinds of sin she has in her relationships with guys, God will forgive her and wipe her slate clean. Reinforce that you will forgive her as well.

  - Hug her and tell her you love her—no matter what!

As you begin walking toward your previously hidden geocache, ask your daughter how it feels to carry the empty backpack.

Break 6—The Geocache
Once you get near your geocache location, go ahead and help your daughter pinpoint the location on your smartphone app or handheld GPS. She will have fun searching for it and will be excited when she finally locates it.

When she has found it, take a seat, and you are ready to go backstage.

🎟 Backstage Pass

Have your daughter read the words on each rock. Explain to her that each word on the rock represents the emotions you hope and pray she has when she stands at the altar on her wedding day.

Take the rock with the word "Respect" on it. Then, read the "SCRIPT"-ure for today's Episode, Ephesians 5:33:

> *"So again I say, a man must love his wife as a part of himself; and the wife must see to it that she deeply respects her husband—obeying, praising, and honoring him." (TLB)*

Point out how the Bible advises wives to deeply respect their husbands. Ask her what she thinks about the fact that the Bible asks men to love their wives and asks wives to respect their husbands.

Going back to our experts, Livy and Shaunti, respectively, now would be a great time to share our experts' advice on the importance of showing guys respect.

"Guys look to the girls they know for respect and affirmation."[4]

"While it may seem odd to most of us, the male need for respect and affirmation—especially from the main girl in his life—is even more important than love."[5]

Let her know that you love her and always want what is best for her. Instead of having the weight of those sinful emotions, you believe it is better to wait to date—even if she has already started dating.

From what you know and have recently learned, it is more beneficial for your daughter to be a great friend to guys before she jumps into a dating relationship. If and when she decides to date, despite your advice, encourage her to establish clear-cut boundaries within the relationship when it comes to physical touch and to make sure she communicate those boundaries with her boyfriend.

Dads, I am going to let you take it from here. The decision to establish your own rules about dating must be well thought out, discussed, and prayed about. You have seen some of the research from our experts. If you thought this Episode was deep, a bit awkward, but absolutely worth it, you will really enjoy the next Episode!

As you might have already noticed, the questions I usually have within the Backstage Pass were included in the 3-2-1 Action! Activity.

Now it's time for the cameras.

🎬 Red Carpet Interview

Red Carpet Questions for Dad

1. Dad, did you have fun hiding the geocache? Why did you pick that spot? Tell me all about it.

2. Who did you talk to about girls and dating when you were a kid?

3. What "weight," if any, did you carry with you on your wedding day?

4. If you could pick one of the sinful emotions from the bricks/rocks in the backpack that you could guarantee that I don't have on my wedding day, what would it be? And why?

5. If you could pick one of the small rocks that you want me to have on my wedding day, what would it be? And why?

Red Carpet Questions for Daughter

1. Was the bag of bricks/rocks too heavy to carry?

2. What was the most important thing you learned about boys or boundaries today?

3. Do you have a better idea about where you want to set boundaries with the guys you date? If you feel comfortable sharing your thoughts, go ahead.

4. What sinful emotion scares you the most about current or future relationships with guys?

5. When you get married, what emotions do you dream about having when you are standing at the altar?

6. How many popcorn buckets would you give today's Episode? (Circle your choice)

 Hannah's Take

A lot of people in my grade have started dating. I am only in eighth grade! I think that in our culture the whole concept of dating gets completely twisted around. Dating is not to just "have fun." Dating is supposed to help us find our future husband.

All the stories I have heard about middle school and even high school girls' boyfriends have been stories of heartbreak or complete embarrassment. To be honest, I really don't want to deal with all of that drama when I am still figuring out who God wants me to be.

We can't let guys define us! We need to let God define us, and He will lead us to know when He wants us to start dating. We all need to be confident in Christ alone.

—Hannah

Who has a geocaching Episode experience they want to share on the *Friday Night Lights for Fathers Private Facebook Group*?

 **Episode 8**   Date: ____ / ____ / _____
A Sticky Situation

 Episode Guide

Theme
Teen Sex

"SCRIPT"-ure

> *Purify me from my sins and I will be clean; wash me, and I will be whiter than snow.*
>
> *Psalm 51:7 NLT*

Set Location
Outside fire pit or kitchen table

3-2-1 Action! Activity
Bonfire and S'mores (outdoors or tabletop)

The Pitch

Let's face it, dads; we live in a sex-driven society. From television (TV) to Target, from the movies to the mall, sex sells. Whether it be the full-sized mural of a half-naked model at Abercrombie & Fitch or the sexual innuendos of Hardee's hamburger commercials, our daughters are inundated with sexual references on a daily basis.

Would you believe, on average, teenagers in the United States view 14,000 sexual references, jokes, and innuendos on TV alone in the course of a year? That's 38 sexual references a day, dads! Additionally, more than 80% of the top teen TV shows contain sexual content.[1]

According to the *American Association of Pediatrics*, our daughters "view more than 3,000 ads per day on TV, on the Internet, on billboards, and in magazines." If that doesn't get you fired up, the same article reveals research is showing that teenagers' exposure to sexual content in the media may be responsible for earlier onset of sexual intercourse or other sexual activities.[2]

If you have been filming your *Friday Night Lights for Fathers and Daughters* reality TV series in order (it's okay if you haven't), you will remember that we just learned about teenage boys. Yes, even though the majority of guys will "check out" a girl who is "hot," that doesn't necessarily make them creepy. We also learned that guys are looking for respect from girls they will eventually date. One more thing that stood out was the importance of having our daughters clearly communicate boundaries in their boyfriend-girlfriend relationships.

But, let's get real—if two teenagers of the opposite sex like each other, find themselves alone, and start kissing, it doesn't take much to move things along toward sex.

I really appreciate Dannah Gresh's question, from her book, *What Are You Waiting For?*

When it comes to contact with your boyfriend, how far is too far?[3]

Go ahead, ask your daughter the question:
When it comes to contact with your boyfriend, how far is too far? (Have your daughter circle where she would draw the line before marriage)

10. Sexual Intercourse

9. Oral Sex

8. Mutual Masturbation

7. Breast Fondling

6. The Horizontal Make-Out

5. The Vertical Make-Out

4. An Open-Mouthed Kiss

3. A Soft Kiss

2. A Heartfelt Hug

1. Holding Hands[3]

An awkward conversation for sure, but talk with your daughter about sexual boundaries. How far is too far to go physically with a guy? This is a great follow-up question to the last Episode.

Well, you might say, "My daughter is still sweet and innocent—we don't have cable TV and don't shop at any of the stores that promote sex." You might also be thinking, "We have given our daughter a purity ring, signed a purity pledge, or have attended a purity ball."

If any of these statements ring true as you read through this Episode, I want to commend you. All of these attempts to limit the sexual references your daughter is exposed to are well worth it. In fact, Jen and I have gone through the Rainey's *Passport to Purity* weekend with both of our kids and have signed the purity pledge with them. We cancelled our cable subscription years ago and limit our shopping at the stores with sexy pictures of teen models. Others of you may have bought your daughter a purity ring or taken her to a purity ball.

Let me be clear; this Episode is not leading up to a purity ring ceremony, a purity pledge, a purity ball, or any of the other wonderful work done by some amazing experts in the field. If you are interested in any of the already established faith-based purity resources on the market, I encourage you to check them out.

Rather, this Episode is about having a conversation with your daughter about how sex before marriage will likely affect her, both physically and emotionally. I have done my best to create an Episode that will be memorable for both you and your daughter, will help illustrate God's plan for sexual purity, while at the same time, reminds all of us that we serve a God who wipes our sins clean, including sexual sin.

In order to set the stage for this Episode, we must know the facts. No, not "the facts of life," because this Episode assumes that you have already had "the talk" or several "talks" with your daughter and that you are continuing to answer her questions about sex as they come up.

Even though you may be doing your best to limit the number of sexual references she is exposed to, the simple fact is that 41% of high school students have sexual intercourse before they graduate high school.[4]

Shall I go on?

The Centers for Disease Control and Prevention (CDC) shows us how quickly girls move from not having sex to having sex.

9th Grade:	20.7% of girls have had sexual intercourse
10th Grade:	33.5% of girls have had sexual intercourse
11th Grade:	48.2% of girls have had sexual intercourse
12th Grade:	57.2% of girls have had sexual intercourse[4]

Despite our best efforts, our teenage girls are still having sex. Purity pledges or not, teen sex still happens.

The main goal of this Episode is to explore effective ways in which we can educate our daughters about sex without objectifying them, without lecturing them, and without scarring them for life.

I took some time to reflect on how my parents taught me about sex. From what I can remember, my parents told me that having sex was one of the best gifts God has given us. They stressed that sex was an expression of love and was a gift to be shared with only the one person you truly loved and wanted to spend the rest of your life with.

I am one of the fortunate ones—my parents showed me a moral compass that, no doubt, pointed me in the right direction and saved me from the onslaught of issues and emotional baggage that teenage sex and sex outside of marriage has proven to cause. Despite these advantages, I still made decisions I regretted.

As dads, we have a responsibility, but also a unique opportunity, to talk to our daughters about what sex is and what sex isn't. And today, that's just what we are going to do.

Let's get right into it!

As you are aware, traditional sex education for teens focuses on the physical risks of sex. While this is certainly important to share with your daughter, I want to add scripture and science to help you inform your daughters about sex. More on scripture and science in a moment, but first, some startling sex statistics we all need to know:

Risks of Sexually Transmitted Diseases

- Until the 1970s, there were only two major types of sexually transmitted diseases: syphilis and gonorrhea. Today there are, at last count, over twenty-five different types of STDs.

    - Among the most common are: syphilis, gonorrhea, HIV/AIDS, human papillomavirus (HPV)—up to 70 different types—and chlamydia.[5]

- Young people (aged 13–24) accounted for an estimated 22% of all new HIV diagnoses in the United States in 2015.[6]

- Half of the nearly 20 million new STDs reported each year were among young people, between the ages of 15 to 24.[6]

- The US has the highest rate of STD infection in the industrialized world.[7]

- 1 in 4 teens contract a sexually transmitted disease every year.[7]

- Sexually active teenage girls who took a pledge of abstinence were at a higher risk of contracting (HPV) than those who did not take such a pledge.[8]

Risks for Unintended Pregnancies

- Nearly 230,000 babies were born to teen girls aged 15–19 in 2015.[6]

- Only 40 percent of teen mothers finish high school. Fewer than 2 percent finish college by age 30.[9]

- Sexually active teenage girls who took a pledge of abstinence were at a higher risk of having non-marital pregnancies than those who did not take such a pledge.[8]

- Only about 10 percent of teen mothers complete a two or four-year college program.[9]

- 80% of teen mothers have to rely on social welfare.[10]

- To further emphasize the impact and emotional risks of teen sex to your daughter, consider this:

  - Sexually active teen girls are more likely to be depressed than their virgin friends. In a study that controlled other factors, researchers found

> that sexually active girls are *three times as likely* to report being depressed as virgins.[11]
>
> - Even more startling and sad was the finding that sexually active girls were three times as likely to have attempted suicide as their virgin counterparts.[11]

These are just a few of the risks that teen sex and sex outside of the marriage you should share with your daughter at some point during today's Episode.

As I mentioned earlier, these statistics are commonly used as scare tactics by parents, public and private schools, and government-funded programs.

As a masters-prepared nurse, I am trained to do research. So, as you can imagine, when I ran across scientific research about the effects of sex, I had to explore.

In 2008, Drs. Joe S. McIlhaney and Freda McKissic Bush published a riveting book titled, *Hooked: New science on how casual sex is affecting our children*. If you want more of an in-depth scientific look into how sex is affecting your daughter, I would encourage you to get this book or their follow-up book, *Girls Uncovered: What America's sexual culture does to young women*.

For now, though, I want to give you the highlights of what these authors have unpacked for us as it relates to the impact of sex and how it affects our teenage daughters' brains.

McIlhaney and McKissic Bush start their book with the following quote:

> "Popular culture would have us believe that young people should become involved in sex when they feel ready, and that with proper precautions, everything will be fine. But the facts tell a different story."[12]

As I read through chapter 1, I couldn't help but be blown away by these words:

> Until now, efforts to accurately assess the connection between love and sex, love, sexual desire, sexual risk-taking, and so on with brain activity have been limited. But with the aid of modern research techniques and technologies, scientists are confirming that sex is more than a momentary physical act. It produces powerful, even lifelong, changes in our brains that direct and influence our future to a surprising degree.[12]

As I read through *Hooked*, I kept wondering if McIlhaney, the lead author, was a Christian. The way he wrote led me to believe he was. After doing a bit of searching, my instincts were right, McIlhaney is a Christian man. Not that it matters, but science supported and confirmed by a Christian scientist always leads me to believe that God continues to reveal His master plan to us over time. Oh, by the way, Dr. McIlhaney and his wife also raised three daughters.

Did you know that your brain is considered a sex organ? If you, like me, answered "no," we are most certainly wrong. Made up of neurons that have over 100 trillion connections, "The human brain is the most complicated 3-pound mass of matter in the universe."[12]

Hooked goes on to inform us that our brains are not completely molded until we turn about 25 years old. The last part of our brains to develop is the prefrontal cortex which is responsible for making mature decisions, setting priorities, organizing plans and ideas, and controlling impulses—something the car rental business has been well aware of for many years.

Stay with me through this scientific journey for a few more minutes; it is so worth it.

Neurochemicals: Dopamine and Oxytocin

Neurochemicals, simply stated, are chemicals that send messages from one brain cell to another to accomplish specific tasks.

Here is the best description I have found to describe the main role of neurochemicals:

> Every millisecond of every day, a remarkable string of events occurs in the brain: billions of brain cells called neurons transmit signals to each other. And they do it at trillions of junctions called synapses. It is an extremely fast and efficient process—one central to everything the brain does, including learning, memorizing, planning, reasoning, and enabling movement.[13]

I invite you to learn about two of the most influential neurochemicals in your daughter's life: dopamine and oxytocin.

Dopamine is a values-neutral neurochemical that rewards its owner for risky behavior—such as skydiving, drinking alcohol, and sex. Despite reaching peak levels in the rest of the brain by late childhood, high levels of dopamine flood the prefrontal cortex during the tween and teen years. Therefore, these high levels of risk-reward neurochemicals are bathing the last of the undeveloped area of our daughters' brains at a time when they are most vulnerable to act on risky behaviors, such as teenage sex.[12]

Because "sex is one of the strongest generators of the dopamine reward," our daughters need our guidance and support during these transformative years. In fact, because of the what McIlhaney and McKessic Bush share next, our daughters can literally get "hooked" on sex.[12]

I would now like to introduce you to dopamine's cousin, oxytocin. You may have heard of a few of the roles oxytocin plays in a woman's body—contractions and breastfeeding/

bonding between mother and child. Most likely, though, you have not heard oxytocin's other roles—the breakthrough neuroscience I want to share with you, and for you to share with your daughter.

Neuroscientists have been able to show the power of oxytocin as it relates to sex. "When two people touch each other in a warm, meaningful way, oxytocin is released into the woman's brain. The oxytocin then does two things: increases a woman's desire for more touch and causes bonding of the woman to the man she has been spending time in physical contact with."[12]

Let's explore this a bit more because it is so critical that our daughters understand these important concepts.

Researchers know that, like dopamine, oxytocin is values-neutral, meaning that it does not distinguish between a fling with a guy or your daughter's true love.[12]

According to the research, the bonding effect is not just an emotional feeling, but actually creates a physiological connection that is "like the *adhesive effect of glue*—a powerful connection that cannot be undone without great emotional pain."[14]

What's even more concerning is that oxytocin cannot distinguish between a one-night stand and a lifelong soul mate. It can cause a woman to bond to a man even during what was expected to be a short-term sexual relationship. "This can lead to a woman being taken off-guard by a desire to stay with him even if he is possessive or abusive."[12]

Check this out: A neuropsychiatrist at the University of California showed how quickly the bonding or "gluing process" of oxytocin begins. Oxytocin was shown to be released in a woman's brain within as little as twenty seconds during a hug between a man and a woman, thus sealing the bond between huggers.[12]

Warning! If you and your daughter get nothing else out of this Episode other than what I am about to share with you next, this Episode will be worth it.

In fact, this warning is also emphasized by the authors of *Hooked*, and it goes like this:

> There is a warning here for parents and young people, ***especially young women***. If a young woman becomes physically close to and hugs a man, it will trigger the bonding process, creating a greater desire to be near him and, most significantly, place greater trust in him. Then, if he wants to escalate the physical nature of the relationship, it will become harder and harder for her to say no.[12]

I could go on and on with statistic after statistic and study after study. I could share more about how neurochemicals bond our daughters with the young men they hug and beyond. However, I believe the bottom line is that we, as dads, must have an open-door policy with our daughters (and sons) when it comes to talking about sex. We must be willing to share not only "the facts of life" with them, but we must be honest in sharing the decisions we made about sex, the current research, and encourage them to wait to have sex until they are married.

Why? Because a twenty-second hug can bond them with a man for life. If a hug can bond them, what effect will multiple sexual partners have on the health of our daughters? I will wrap up with a quote from McIlhaney and McKessic Bush. They were able to say in one paragraph what I have been trying to say in several pages:

> It appears that the most up-to-date research suggests that most humans are 'designed' to be sexually monogamous with one mate for life. This information also shows that the more we deviate from this behavior, the more problems they encounter; STDs, nonmarital pregnancy, or emotional problems, including damaged ability to

develop healthy connectedness with others, including future spouses.[12]

Your daughter might also find it comforting to know that most young people (90%) think it is best to remain abstinent until they are married.[12]

Behind the Scenes Setup (for Dad)

Set Location
Campfire in your own backyard, local park, or at your kitchen table (seriously!)

3-2-1 Action! Activity Overview
For those of you that know me well, it may come as a surprise to you that one of my greatest childhood memories is sitting around the campfire "on the rocks" at Camp Van Vac in Ely, Minnesota. On the edge of the Boundary Waters Canoe Area (BWCA), my parents, sisters, aunts, uncles, cousins, and others would grab a spot on the rocks and listen to my cousin Paige play her guitar and sing campfire songs.

We would spray ourselves with copious amounts of bug spray, listen to Paige sing, and stare at the dancing flames of the campfire, all under a sky full of stars.

There's just something soothing about a fire that invites deeper conversations. Oh, and who doesn't love roasting marshmallows and making those gooey, sticky, and delightful campfire favorite, S'mores?

Besides providing a calming and thought-provoking atmosphere, our campfire will allow you to create the illustration of the stickiness that physical contact and sex causes in the minds and hearts of your daughter.

Before we can start The Live Shoot! though, we need to gather our materials for the Stage Checklist.

Stage Checklist

- Schedule today's Live Shoot! with your daughter and put it on your calendar.

- Choose your campfire location
    - Backyard fire pit, local park fire pit, or your kitchen table (not a typo!)

- Matches or a lighter

- Firestarter or kindling/paper

- Graham crackers, a bag of marshmallows, and a couple of chocolate candy bars

- Firewood that will last at least one hour
    - Approximately one bundle of firewood at your local gas station

- Cold Weather Campfire Stage Checklist
    - Firewood options
        - Traditional firewood bundle
        - One-log campfire
            - TimberTote.com on Amazon, at Lowe's, ACE Hardware, or other hardware or camping stores (Minnesota-based!)
    - Table-top S'mores options:
        - Nostalgia S'mores Maker
        - Sterno S'mores Maker
        - Simple Stovetop S'mores recipe from BuzzFeed: http://bit.ly/stovetopsmores

🎬 The Live Shoot!

Pre-Episode Prayer

Heavenly Father,

Sex is a wonderful gift that you have given us to share inside the covenant of marriage. As _____ (daughter's name) and I begin our discussion on sex, help me to choose the words You want me to use and help _____ (daughter's name) understand the message I am doing my best to teach her. The pressure for sex is all around us. Help me to convey Your message about sex to her without instilling a sense of guilt or shame about sex. Help me to balance the true reasons for waiting until marriage for sex with the excitement and joy of sex within a marriage. We both need Your help during today's Episode and pray that You give us patience and understanding as we talk.

In Jesus' name we pray,
Amen

3-2-1 Action! Activity

We would all agree that talking to our daughters about sex is a bit awkward—okay, super awkward. We have learned a great deal about what takes place in our daughter's brains when it comes to something as simple as hugging her boyfriend, let alone having sex with him.

We also know that sexual sins are some of the most emotionally-charged and culturally objectified sins our daughters might endure.

So, instead of objectifying sex as a "gift" our daughters may or may not choose, instead of laying guilt on them if they break their purity pledge or tarnish their purity ring because they decided to have sex, let's give them the facts. In a loving and truthful way, let's provide them with the latest research, the most recent statistics, and most importantly, Scripture.

Dads, I know this is tough, and you might be nervous, but I am confident that you can do this with God's help.

Once you have prayed together and have started your campfire, whether it be on a warm summer evening, a frigid winter night, or at your kitchen table, start asking your daughter the following questions:

1. Have any of your friends ever talked about having sex? (If she answers 'No,' skip to question #4.)

2. How did that make you feel?

3. Did it make you feel pressured into having sex?

4. In what ways does culture affect you as it relates to sex?

5. What are your thoughts about having sex before you get married?

When she has answered, ask her why she chose her particular answer.

6. Next, share some of the statistics about teen pregnancy from The Pitch. Here are a few key points to get you started

   - 41% of all high schoolers have had sex before graduating from high school

   - 9th Grade: 20.7% of girls have had sexual intercourse
   10th Grade: 33.5% of girls have had sexual intercourse

11th Grade: 48.2% of girls have had sexual intercourse
12th Grade: 57.2% of girls have had sexual intercourse

- Only 40 percent of teen mothers finish high school. Fewer than 2 percent finish college by age 30.

- 1 in 4 teens contract a sexually transmitted disease every year.

- Here are a few words girls use to describe how they feel after they have sex for the first time: dirty, disgusting, used, naughty, and depressed

- Sexually active teen girls are more likely to be depressed than their virgin friends—sexually active girls are *three times as likely* to report being depressed as virgins.

- New research shows that neurochemicals (mainly oxytocin) creates long-term bonds between partners who do anything from hugging each other for 20 seconds to having sex. The bond may last a lifetime and is extremely painful to break, even if the guy is a jerk.

7. Ask your daughter what statistic shocked her the most and why?

8. Next, share the information about the neurochemicals dopamine and oxytocin. Feel free to go back and re-read the entire section on Neurochemicals: Dopamine and Oxytocin. Otherwise, I have summarized the information in the following bullet points:

- Did you know that your brain is a sex organ—made up of neurons that have over 100 trillion connections, "The human brain is the most complicated 3-pound mass of matter in the universe."

- Your brain communicates through neurochemicals, which are chemicals that send messages from one brain cell to another to accomplish specific tasks.

- Two neurochemicals I want to talk about today are dopamine and oxytocin:

  - Dopamine is known as the "risk-reward" neurochemical and is at its highest levels during your teenage years. It may cause you to make sexual decisions based on risk rather than your boundaries.

  - Oxytocin is known as the "bonding" neurochemical. Oxytocin is most prevalent in women and helps develop bonding between mother and baby.

    - However, new brain science has shown that oxytocin can cause life-long emotional bonds with guys you have sex with. In fact, these bonds, described as "glue" or "an adhesive," can form simply after hugging a guy for twenty seconds.

    - These bonds with boyfriends, one-night stands, or hugging have been proven to last a lifetime and may seriously affect future relationships, even marriages.

- Finally, you must also understand that these neurochemicals are values-neutral, meaning that they can't tell the difference between a fling or a serious relationship. They can't tell the difference between a loving relationship or an abusive relationship. These sticky, lifelong bonds form when you engage in physical touch with a guy.

9. Allow your daughter to absorb this new information for a couple of minutes. Clarify any questions she may have. Then, when she is ready, move on to Step 10.

10. Get out your S'mores supplies. This is where things get real, dads.

    a. Both you and your daughter will roast at least one marshmallow.

    b. Once the marshmallow is roasted, sandwich it with a piece of chocolate between two graham crackers. Make sure the chocolate has a few seconds to melt into the marshmallow.

11. Before your daughter dives into this delicious treat, ask her to give you back the piece of chocolate.

12. Obviously, she will not be able to because it will have started melting. She will give you that confused look. It is now time for the reveal.

🎟 Backstage Pass

By now, both you and your daughter's fingers are messy from trying to separate the melting chocolate and the sticky marshmallow. And that's just the point, right—some things cannot be undone.

The chocolate and the marshmallow have become one. It didn't take long, maybe 20 seconds or so, but neither will be the same.

Much like when a girlfriend and boyfriend cross a boundary of physical touch. Whether it be a 20-second hug, a kiss, or maybe even sex, the neurochemicals in our brain create a sticky bond between the relationship that has been scientifically proven to last a lifetime.

At this point dads, I would recommend reading the warning that our experts shared with us earlier:

> If a young woman becomes physically close to and hugs a man, it will trigger the bonding process, creating a greater desire to be near him and, most significantly, place greater trust in him. Then, if he wants to escalate the physical nature of the relationship, it will become harder and harder for her to say no.[12]

This isn't just something new to the 21st century. Check out what Paul had to say to Timothy nearly 2,000 years ago:

"Now flee from youthful lusts, and pursue righteousness, faith, love, and peace, with those who call on the Lord from a pure heart." (2 Timothy 2:22) What a perfect verse that continues to withstand the test of time.

Despite all of the pressures our culture places on sexuality, especially aimed at our daughters, I love that we serve a God who not only forgives us when we make mistakes but helps us to prevent those same mistakes with wise words of wisdom.

As fathers to daughters, I believe we must share both science and Scripture with our daughters when it comes to discussing sex. Today, dad, you have done just that.

🎀 Red Carpet Interview

Red Carpet Questions for Dad

1. Dad, did you ever have a "Sex Talk" like this with your parents? Tell me a little bit about it.

2. Of all of the information you talked about today, what one piece of information would you have liked to have known when you were a teenager?

3. Who did you feel most comfortable talking to about sex when you were a teenager? Why?

4. Do you think I can wait until marriage until I have sex?

Red Carpet Questions for Daughter

1. What is the most surprising thing you learned about sex today?

2. Be as honest as you can—on a scale of 1–100, with 100 being super awkward, and 1 being not awkward at all, how would you rate today's talk on sex? Honestly!

3. After today's Episode, did you change your mind at all about when you want to have sex for the first time? Why? What influenced you most?

4. What was your favorite thing about today's Episode?

5. How many popcorn buckets would you give today's Episode? (Circle your choice)

🎬 Hannah's Take

This can be a very awkward thing to discuss, but God created sex to be between a *married* man and woman. It is not supposed to be something you do to show that you love your boyfriend or anything like that. It is a gift from God.

When God guides us to start dating, we will all probably feel temptations. We need to recognize those temptations, and we need to remember how much more important God's precious gift is to us than giving in to sin is.

God will give us the strength to stay true to Him. We need to be confident in Christ and be defined by Him so that we are not swayed by the evil ways of this world. Truly treasure your relationship with God because He will give you the strength to stand strong in Him.

—Hannah

Let's hear those s'mores stories in the *Friday Night Lights for Fathers Private Facebook Group.*

🎬 Episode 9
Draw Near

Date: ____ / ____ / _____

⚙️ Episode Guide

Theme
Prayer

"SCRIPT"-ure

> *Call to me and I will answer you, and will tell you great and hidden things that you have not known.*
>
> *Jeremiah 33:3*

Set Location
Kitchen Table

3-2-1 Action! Activity
Create Prayer Journals

The Pitch

Several years ago, a medic was serving as a missionary in an isolated area of Africa. Because the area was so remote, this missionary medic had to ride his bike several miles through the jungle to the closest town to get needed medical supplies.

After witnessing a fight between two men, the missionary medic treated one of the man's wounds and witnessed to him. After their encounter, they both went their separate ways—or so the missionary medic thought.

A few weeks later, the injured man in the fight approached the missionary medic and told him the following:

I know you carry money and medicine. Some friends and I followed you into the jungle the night you treated me, knowing that you would camp overnight. We waited for you to go to sleep and planned to kill you and take your money and drugs.

The injured man continued, "Just as we started moving into the campsite, we saw you were surrounded by 26 armed guards. There were only six of us and we knew we couldn't possibly get near you, so we left."

The missionary medic laughed and ensured his former patient that he was definitely alone in the campsite.

The other man argued, "No, sir, I was not the only one to see the guards. My friends also saw them, and we all counted them. We were frightened. It was because of those guards that we left you alone."

The story might have easily ended there, however, a few months later, the truth of the 26 guards was revealed in a rather stunning way.

After the missionary returned home several months later, as was customary, he shared his missionary experiences with his congregants. While he was sharing the story about the 26 guards, one of the members of the audience jumped up and interrupted the missionary's presentation and said:

We were with you in spirit. On that night in Africa, it was morning here. I stopped at the church to gather some material for an out-of-town trip to another parish. But as I put my bags into the trunk, I felt the Lord leading me to pray for you. The urging was so great I called the men of the church together to pray for you.[1]

The man then turned to the congregation and asked, "Will all of those men who met with the Lord that morning please stand up?"

One-by-one, 26 men stood![1]

Prayer works.

You will by now have noticed that before I have you begin each Live Shoot!, I have encouraged you to pray with your daughter before each Episode. I hope that you have not skipped over this valuable time to connect with our Living God.

If you were to ask me to choose one section that is vital to each Episode, my answer, without hesitation, would be the Pre-Episode Prayer.

Why? Because you are modeling the importance of prayer to your daughter on a consistent basis. Because you and your daughter are connecting with the Almighty by simply stating, "Heavenly Father." Because our daughters must know that it is just as important to pray in good times as well as the bad ones.

Unfortunately, many of us dads don't make time for prayer. We are not disciplined enough. We are too busy. We believe that we don't need prayer because we think we can solve our issues on our own. You name it; we dads often feel we can work through our own struggles without asking others for help, especially God.

The truth is, we, just like our daughters, are missing out on one of the most powerful tools any of us could possibly dream about in our toolbox when we leave prayer out.

Not only do we need to reexamine our own prayer lives, but I want to encourage you to assist your daughter in developing a prayer routine with passion and discipline to help her create a strong foundation of prayer throughout her life.

Instead of pretending to understand how our daughters' minds think about prayer, I want to again call on a few experts that know a lot more about this topic than I could ever imagine.

For this Episode, I have called on Jamie, Elizabeth, Marian, and Paige to help us develop a foundation of lifelong prayer in our daughters' lives.

Jamie

In 2015, our family did something we had never done before—we went to an outdoor Christian music festival, The Joyful Noise Family Fest—organized by KTIS 98.5 FM out of the Twin Cities in Minnesota. With a lineup of Christian recording artists, we had our sights set on TobyMac. We had been listening more and more to Christian music but were not prepared for the impact that one of the artists would have on Hannah.

When Jamie Grace took the stage, we were all blown away by her performance, but also by the words of her testimony and her message to young women. Hannah heard her message and was compelled to stand in the hour-plus autograph line just to meet Jamie.

It was well worth the wait for Hannah. As Hannah handed Jamie her poster for an autograph, Jamie's eyes lit up, she smiled at Hannah, and you could tell that Hannah felt like she and Jamie were the only two people in the room. Jamie then spoke these words to Hannah, "You have a beautiful smile and something I always wished I had—freckles. They are beautiful. Be proud of them!"

Since that day, Hannah has never again been self-conscious about her freckles. In fact, because of Jamie Grace, she now sees them as a part of her unique beauty.

Okay, okay this story really has nothing to do with prayer, but I wanted to share it with you because I believe Jamie Grace's words about prayer in her interview with Livy Jarmusch of *Crown of Beauty Magazine* below will both resonate and inspire your daughter to pray consistently.

The Lord hears our every cry, our every prayer. The loud ones, soft ones, deep ones, articulate and random. Whatever is on your heart, whatever may be weighing you down . . . you don't have to find the answer or resolve in a friend, boy, school, job, app, or anything but the peace in knowing the Creator of the beat of your heart is waiting to hear your every word.[2]

What awesome words to share with your daughter about prayer "knowing the Creator of the beat of your heart is waiting to hear your every word."

Thank you, Jamie Grace. Check out her song, *Sixteen*, on iTunes.

Elizabeth

Next, I want to bring in our next prayer expert, Elizabeth George. In her book, *A Young Woman's Guide to Prayer*, Elizabeth shares her rendition of "God's Formula for Effective Prayer":

1. Get Organized!

   - Pick a private place and a consistent time to pray each day.

2. Get Ready!

   Prepare by thinking about your prayer time . . . about how much you look forward to it, about how important prayer is to your spiritual growth, about how crucial it is that your loved ones be prayed for, about the sheer joy of being obedient in this commanded spiritual discipline, about the unbelievable privilege you have to commune with and worship God in this most intimate way.[3]

   - Memorize the "SCRIPT"-ure for today's Episode, Jeremiah 33:3—*Call to me and I will answer you, and will tell you great and hidden things that you have not known.*

> - Elizabeth George refers to Jeremiah 33:3 as God's phone number, much like 9-1-1. In times of emergency, we can call JER333 and be instantly connected with God.[3]

3. Get Up!

> - Sounds simple, right? But how many times do you have good intentions of getting up early only to hit the snooze button multiple times with just enough time to get to work or school?

Elizabeth goes on to stress the importance of having a prayer journal or notebook, noting that her notebook has been her "...Number One mainstay and prayer tool for the 25-plus years she's been on her personal prayer journey."[3]

Marian
Marian Jordan Ellis, the founder of Redeemed Girl Ministries, believes God's best is worth praying for. Marian shares her seven truths about becoming a woman of prayer:

1. Prayer is best when it is raw, messy, and honest.

2. We have not because we ask not. (Matthew 7:7)

3. God's delays are not God's denials.

4. Prayer + The Word go hand in hand.

5. Keep a prayer journal.

6. When we can't understand His hand, we trust His heart.

7. God's best is worth praying for.[4]

Marian understands the power of prayer journals. She reveals that she has 15 years-worth of prayer journals that are a constant reminder of how God has answered her prayers.

Paige

I remember reading about Paige several years ago, even though I didn't know her name and neither did her husband, nor her mother-in-law. Why? You might ask. Well, I first read about Paige in a book on how to pray for your children, by Paige's mother-in-law, Stormie.

Stormie Omartian helped me understand how powerful praying over my children is. In her book, *Power of a Praying Parent*, Stormie shares how she prayed for her son's future spouse from the time he was born.

Her son's future spouse turned out to be Paige, our next expert on teen girls' prayer. It just so happens that Paige co-authored a book with Stormie, titled, *A Book of Prayers for Young Women*, in which she shares prayers that matter to girls of the 21st century in a culture that seems to oppose Christ at every corner.

A Book of Prayers for Young Women contains prayers such as "I Need Godly Friends" and "Show Me My Purpose" to "Waiting for My Husband" and "Transforming My Life." In total, Stormie and Paige have put together 154 applicable prayers for your daughter.

There you have it—prayer advice for your daughter from four experts in the field.

As I reviewed each of the experts' advice on prayer for our daughters, a couple of themes emerged that I believe we should share with our daughters during today's Episode.

- There is no right or wrong way to pray
- Consistent prayer requires a plan
- God always listens
- God's best is worth praying for
- There is power in prayer
- Prayer journals reveal answered prayers

☒ Behind the Scenes Setup (for Dad)

Set Location
Home

3-2-1 Action! Activity Overview
You and your daughter will each be creating your own prayer journals. While applying our experts' advice, you will also be setting up a prayer plan to hold each other accountable.

Stage Checklist
Please know that you and your daughter may be as creative as possible for today's 3-2-1 Action! Activity, and may purchase any type of notebook and decorating tools as you wish. However, the Stage Checklist includes the basic items necessary to create a simple, yet powerful prayer journal.

- Composition notebooks - 100 pages (2)
- Scrapbook paper - enough for two journals (optional)
- Mod-Podge or glue
- Scissors
- Clear tape
- Color Markers
- Filing Tabs - minimum of 12 individual tabs (optional)

🎥 The Live Shoot!

Pre-Episode Prayer

Heavenly Father,

Thank you for the time that _____ (daughter's name) and I have today. We are so grateful that we serve a living God that who communicates directly with us. Help us both to develop a passion for prayer, knowing that You listen to our every word, that You answer every prayer, and that You delight in our relationship with You. Jeremiah 33:3 says that if we call out to You, You will answer us and will tell us great and hidden things we didn't know. Help us to understand that Your best is worth praying for. Help us to develop a plan to pray each and every day and to have the discipline to write down our prayers and thoughts in a prayer journal. Last, help me to lead _____ (daughter's name) to a life filled with the power of prayer.

In Jesus' name we pray,
Amen

3-2-1 Action! Activity

Craft projects usually don't make my top 10 list of things to do, but I know that my daughter loves crafts. So, during today's Episode, you and your daughter will both create your very own personally customized prayer journal.

I searched high and low for a simple yet effective prayer journal that will motivate both you and your daughter to begin praying today—and I found it, thanks to Ashley Roe, a contributor at YoungWifesGuide.com and Molly Garibaldi at ThroneofGrace.com.

Take your daughter to the nearest hobby shop or big box shopping store to pick up the Stage Checklist supplies. If you choose to use scrapbook paper, your daughter will most likely want to pick out her own design.

The color and design of your prayer journal should be something that inspires you and invites you to open it. Have fun with it and be as creative as possible.

1. Once you have all of your supplies, pick a spot in your home where you can get a bit messy. Lay out all of your supplies and start thinking about how you would like to design your cover. Here are a couple of ideas to get you and your daughter thinking:

   - Favorite Bible verse

   - Your "My One Word"

   - Picture of you and your daughter

   - Drawing or picture of a cross

2. Next, if you are using scrapbook paper, you will need to measure out the paper to ensure you can cover the composition notebook.

3. Once you have cut the scrapbook paper to size, line it up and spread the Mod-Podge over the surface of the scrapbook paper. Make sure to smooth out the surface as much as possible before the adhesive dries. You may want to apply a second coat once the first one dries. If you use glue, just apply glue onto the surface of the composition notebook and place the scrapbook paper on.

4. Filing tabs - You can either choose to make tabs with the scrapbook paper or purchase them. Either way, you will need at least six per prayer journal.

a. Cut scrapbook paper about 2 inches by 2 inches. Fold them in half and write the following words on separate tabs:

- Thanks for

- Sorry for

- Please

- Family

- Friends

- Others

b. Next, split up your pages as evenly as you can.

c. Then, place your tabs on the first page of each section.

d. Lastly, place each tab in descending order so that there is a tab on the first page. To attach, unfold the tab and tape it to one piece of paper. Fold over and tape the other side to the back of that same piece of paper. Be sure that you have enough room to leave the label visible when the notebook is closed.

5. On the inside cover of the prayer journal, write you're "My One Word" as a daily reminder of the word that God put on your heart during the Believe Episode.

6. Congratulations! You did it. Both you and your daughter now have a prayer journal.

Once you and your daughter have admired the amazing craftsmanship of your recently completed customized prayer journals, it is now time to talk about the power of prayer, develop a prayer plan, and discuss what to write about inside of your new creation.

Review our experts' advice on why developing a daily prayer life is so important in our walk with God.

- Jamie Grace: God listens to your every word.

- Elizabeth George: Get Ready. Get Organized. Get Up.

- Marian Jordan Ellis: God's best is worth praying for.

- Paige Omartian: Pray even though the 21st-century culture seems to oppose Christ at every corner.

Here are some tips Molly Garabaldi suggests writing about in each of the 6 prayer journal tabs:

- **"Thanks for . . ."** – A section for praise and adoration of God and His faithfulness. Here you can record blessings, thoughts of gratitude, and answered prayers.

- **"Sorry for . . ."** – This tab is set up for confession of sin – both sins of commission (choosing to do wrong) and sins of omission (NOT choosing to do what is right).

- **"Please . . ."** – Use this section to record your own prayer requests. What do you need or desire from the Lord? He wants us to ask boldly, meaning with a lot of faith, yet humbly – recognizing that He is God and we are not! Ask the Lord to help you line up your desires with His desires.

- **"Family"** – Prayers for your family members.

- **"Friends"** – Prayers for friends.

- **"Others"** – Prayers for anyone else God puts on your heart to pray for – teachers, coaches, pastors, neighbors, missionaries, our country's leaders—even your enemies![5]

Before each entry, make sure to date your entries. This way, you can go back in time and see how God's faithfulness to answered prayer has impacted your life.

Keep your prayers simple so that you can continue to meditate, or think about, those prayers throughout your day.

Keep your prayers specific so that when God answers, you will clearly see His work in your life.

Don't worry about how much you write. Some days when you have more time you might write half a page in each section, some days just a few lines, and maybe some days you just read through what you've already written, and pray over that.[5]

You and your daughter should also plan a time to pray and write in your journals each day.

One of our prayer journal experts, Elizabeth George, suggests that we pray to get up to pray and to think of the phrase "mind over mattress"—and goes on to say, "This must become your response to your alarm's sound. Treat it like it is God calling you to prayer. It's your Commander-in-Chief. It's the Ruler of your life. It's the Master bidding you to join Him in prayer. So . . . get up!"[3]

Finally, challenge your daughter to set an alarm for 15 minutes (or more) earlier than normal on the following day to start her daily prayer plan and journal. By the way, Dad, that means you, too.

⊞ Backstage Pass

For this Episode's Backstage Pass, go ahead and interject the following questions about prayer into your conversation as you are creating your customized prayer journals.

1. How often would you say you pray?

2. Do you think God answers all prayers?

3. What do you pray most about?

4. Can you tell me about a prayer that you believe God has answered?

5. How about a prayer that God didn't answer?

6. Have you always been happy with God's answers to your prayers?

7. Are you worried that prayer has to be formal and perfect, using big church words?

8. What do you think prevents you from praying more or from praying at all?

Don't read each question back-to-back, but allow your daughter the time to answer each question—then respond with love and support.

Once you have completed your journals and have asked all of the Backstage Pass questions, it's time to roll out the Red Carpet!

🎗 Red Carpet Interview

Red Carpet Questions for Dad

1. All right Dad, be honest with me, how often do you pray?

2. Do you pray for me? If so, what do you pray for?

3. When it is my day to pray about you, Dad, what would you like me to pray about?

4. Dad, if you don't already, will you pray for me about _____? (daughter's prayer request)

5. How would you rate my new prayer journal on a scale of 1–10?

Red Carpet Questions for Daughter

1. _____ (daughter's name), which one of our experts did you feel had the best advice for you personally?

2. Can you recite today's "SCRIPT"-ure for me? Hint: It is Jeremiah 33:3 (Here it is if you need it: *Call to me and I will answer you, and will tell you great and hidden things that you have not known.*)

3. A. (If you currently pray for your daughter): Were you surprised that I prayed for you? What surprised you the most and why? B. (If you would like to start praying for your daughter): Would you like me to start praying for you? Why?

4. Do you have any other questions about prayer that you would like to ask me about or that you are still unsure of?

5. How many popcorn buckets would you give today's Episode? (Circle your choice)

Hannah's Take

God created us to have a personal relationship with Him. Praying is very important because it is how we talk to God and grow in our relationship with Him!

Sometimes, we can think that our prayers have to be well thought out and that we need to say exactly the right words. That is not true! God knows exactly what we mean when we pray. He knows our thoughts, our feelings, and everything about us. (Psalm 139:2)

How we talk to God is different for all of us, so if the prayer journal just doesn't work for you, try something different. There are many different things to help guide you with how to pray. Just remember that God wants to hear from you, no matter what. He wants you to talk to Him like you are talking to your best friend.

—Hannah

Let's fill the *Friday Night Lights for Fathers Private Facebook Group* with pictures of you and your daughters brand-new prayer journals. Every post will help encourage other dads and daughters to make their own.

 # Season Finale

Date: ____ / ____ / _____

Woman of Valor

 ## Episode Guide

Theme
Valor

"SCRIPT"-ure

> *A woman of valor who can find?*
>
> *Proverbs 31:10 JPS*

Set Location
Your Daughter's Favorite Restaurant

3-2-1 Action! Activity
Dinner on Dad

The Pitch

In our quest to be the best dads to our daughters, we look to Jesus Christ, the only man to walk this world without sin. We can only do our best to live a Christ-like life. Why? Because we are broken. When Adam took a bite of the forbidden fruit, our opportunity for being perfect was squandered. Even so, we do our best each and every day to be the dads we were designed to be, we strive to live a sin-free life but, let's be honest, we all fall short.

And so, it is with our daughters as they look to the image of the Proverbs 31 woman. The lessons that King Lemuel shared from his mother in Proverbs 31 paints a picture of what our daughters can aspire to. The key to the last statement is "aspire to," not "to perfect."

While many believe that Proverbs 31 is the definition of biblical womanhood, many would argue that it is actually detrimental to women—portraying the perfect woman no woman could possibly ever measure up to.

The Proverbs 31 Woman, taken literally, describes a woman who may seem almost super-human to our daughters. This is ludicrous, just as if we require our sons and our young men to become just like Jesus.

Rather, I believe the words of Proverbs 31 help cast a vision for our daughters as to what they can aspire to as women of God.

When I first decided to write this book, I knew that I wanted Proverbs 31 to be an integral part of the book. As I approached this particular season finale Episode, I kept feeling strong resistance to Proverbs 31. I literally spent weeks searching for other ways to wrap up an awesome season with my daughter. I read more material for this particular Episode than any other in the entire book.

I prayed to the Holy Spirit for guidance, discernment, and wisdom on how to message this Episode. Finally, just about to throw in the towel, I felt led to walk upstairs and ask Hannah what, if any, ideas she had for the topic and message for the final Episode.

I asked Hannah the question, and she said, "Let me think about it." I thanked her for listening and started back on my endless Google searches for new ideas on how to end the season with a meaningful message.

To my surprise, Hannah started to speak about ten minutes later. She said, "Dad, you know what I think you should write about?" I shook my head, eagerly awaiting her answer. She went on, "I think you should write about Proverbs 31."

I definitely did not expect her to come up with Proverbs 31. I had made every argument for *not* using Proverbs 31. I admit that I used Proverbs 31 to define biblical womanhood in my first book, *Friday Night Lights for Fathers and Sons.*

Caught up in my own thoughts, I soon realized I was wearing my emotions on my sleeve, so Hannah said, "What's wrong, Dad?"

Being the loving dad that I am, I answered her question with a question. "Hannah, how did you come up with your answer?" Without skipping a beat, Hannah replied, "I prayed about it, and Proverbs 31 popped right into my head."

As I do every time I sit down to write, I whispered a little prayer for guidance and wisdom. Within moments, God answered my prayers. This Holy Spirit-led answer is the subject of our season finale Episode!

Lost in Translation

Over the years, many words or phrases have been lost in translation. Take for instance these marketing blunders:

- Burger King's "PooPoo Smoothie"—A mango-flavored bubble tea in China.

- "Barf Soap"—An Iranian detergent that means "snow" in the Farsi language.

- The "Fart Bar"—In Poland, where this candy bar is made, the name translates to "lucky bar."

- "Pee Cola"—Bottled in Ghana—refreshing!

- Chevy Nova—Translated from English to Spanish literally means "No go."[1]

My favorite has to be "Barf Soap." Which is yours?

It is only logical then that a word translated from the ancient Hebrew language to modern-day English might be lost in translation. And, so it is with the Hebrew phrase אֵשֶׁת-חַיִל (eshet chayil), one of the most well-known scriptures on biblical womanhood, Proverbs 31:10.

In the majority of contemporary Bible versions, eshet chayil, is translated into "a virtuous woman" (KJV), "a wife of noble character" (NIV), or "a good wife" (NLT). However, the Jewish Orthodox Bible has stayed, well, orthodox, in its translation of eshet chayil. The Jewish Orthodox Bible continues to translate eshet chayil as, "woman of valor."

In fact, Marilynn Chadwick, author of *Woman of Valor*, shares that, still today, some Jews and Messianic Jews continue to honor their women of valor:

> Every Friday evening before Shabbat, the husband will recite or sing the poem "A Woman of Valor" to honor his wife—to reflect upon and be thankful for all she has done for him, their family, and for the community throughout the past week.[2]

Dads, if you aren't aware of the so-called job description depicted in Proverbs 31, I encourage you to take a moment and read Proverbs 31:10–31 for a quick overview and understanding.

Chadwick describes both her and many other Christian women's thoughts on Proverbs 31:

> Now, I confess that Proverbs 31—with its lengthy tribute to the celebrated virtuous woman—had become a tired, overworked passage of Scripture for me. Or maybe it just made me feel tired and overworked to read about her. Regrettably, the account of this remarkable woman morphed, over the centuries, into a sort of "to-do" list. A job description for the Christian woman that left many feeling inadequate and more than a little exhausted. Honestly, who can be an amazing wife, mother, and homemaker, and run several businesses, serve the poor, and be honored in her city all at the same time? Additionally, some of the commentaries on the Proverbs 31 woman

emphasized only her role as nurturer and manager of her home and family. They seemed to leave out her warrior side altogether.[2]

As I read this passage, something clicked within my heart. I knew immediately why God put Proverbs 31 on Hannah's heart when I asked her what the final Episode's theme should be.

Why? Because rather than focusing on the "nurturer role" of the virtuous translation, the woman of valor translation adds a "warrior role" to the description.

This is a game-changer, not only for our wives and the women of the church but for our daughters as well. When we help our daughters define biblical womanhood as part nurturer and part warrior, we are now seeing the true vision God had when he created Eve. No longer just a virtuous wife, but now a woman of valor.

I can honestly say that I am much more excited to walk alongside my daughter as she transitions from a girl to a young woman with the vision of her becoming both a nurturer and a warrior. What a powerful message we can instill in our daughters. What a powerful message we should instill in our daughters.

Dads. Guess what? For the past nine Episodes of *Friday Night Lights for Fathers and Daughters*, you have been doing just that. Let me show you how.

During the Pilot Episode, you helped teach your daughter about establishing a firm faith foundation. You each chose your "My One Word" and planted the seeds of choosing a life verse.

In the "S.I. vs. S-I" Episode, besides baking an amazing apple pie, you instilled a new confidence in your daughter. Using scripture and facts, you showed her how she was created exactly as God planned it—down to the exact number of hairs on her head.

You helped your daughter differentiate between true, godly friendships and frenemyships.

Despite living in a social media-crazed culture, you helped your daughter create Social Media Guardrails in the "Navigating the Social Media Maze" Episode.

Next, you encouraged your daughter to dream big and then do it! Whether your daughter wants to be a brain surgeon or a pro basketball player, you helped her cast a vision of God's calling for her.

In the "Grattitude" Episode, you, along with 14-year-old Anne Frank, helped squash the entitlement virus that is sweeping our youth. You helped teach your daughter how to have a grateful attitude for what she has been blessed with.

Stick with me here, dads, you have accomplished so much.

During "A Sticky Situation," you learned not just about what scripture has to say about dating and physical contact between your daughter and teen boys, but also what God has been revealing, bit-by-bit, through science.

Moving toward the final Episode, after explaining the pros and cons of purity, whether or not she would rather wait to have sex until her wedding night or if she would rather carry the weight of having sex outside of marriage. This was a challenging conversation, but you did it, Dad!

During the ninth Episode, you encouraged your daughter to "Draw Near and Pray" on a consistent basis. Both of you created prayer journals and are now holding each other accountable to prayer in your daily lives.

You have demonstrated and described to your daughter, through activities, scripture, and dialogue, the description of the Proverbs 31 woman—a woman of valor (part nurturer and part warrior).

Tonight, you will properly translate Proverbs 31:10 for your daughter and will continue to help her transition from a girl to a young woman who is part nurturer and part warrior.

The life-lessons you have taken your daughter through during this *Friday Night Lights for Fathers and Daughters* season, whether you realize it yet or not, have helped lead your daughter in her young adult life. You have helped her connect the dots between the latest scientific research and the God-breathed lessons from scripture.

You have used your particular set of skills uniquely created for fathers only. You now know your daughter better than you did before you filmed your pilot Episode. Your daughter now knows you better than before. Your daughter also knows a bit more about what the boys and young men are thinking about and what they really want in a relationship. My prayer for the both of you is that you have both grown closer to God in the process.

So, tonight, celebrate!

Behind the Scenes Setup (for Dad)

Set Location

The Set Location for the season finale Episode will be your daughter's favorite restaurant. Dads, no persuading her here. Even if you absolutely know what her favorite restaurant is, still confirm it with her.

Whether it is a 5-star or a fast-food restaurant, go with it.

3-2-1 Action! Activity Overview

The goal of the final Episode's activity is three-fold—celebrate a successful season of father/daughter bonding, to paint your daughter a picture of the Proverbs 31:10 woman of valor, and to demonstrate how a gentleman respects a woman on a date. No pressure, dads; this Episode is going to be a blast. You will create a memory that will last a lifetime.

Stage Checklist

- Formally ask your daughter to dinner.

- Confirm your daughter's favorite restaurant and make a reservation, if necessary.

- Schedule The Live Shoot! with your daughter and put in on your calendar.

- (Optional, but encouraged)

  - Make sure you have dress clothes, cleaned, ironed, and ready to wear. A tie would be a nice addition.

  - Ask your wife, daughter's mother, girlfriend, or big sister, if she can take your daughter shopping for a new outfit. Make sure you pay for it.

  - If you wish, take your daughter shopping yourself.

  - Order a corsage and make sure you pick it up in time for your night out.

- Bibles (yours and your daughter's)

- Highlighter and black pen

- 5x7 frame for a photo of you and your daughter at dinner.

🎥 The Live Shoot!

I encourage you to take a couple of minutes before you embark on your season finale Episode and pray the Pre-Episode Prayer below.

Pre-Episode Prayer

Heavenly Father,

Wow! How can it already be our season finale Episode? _____ (daughter's name) and I are so grateful for the time we have had together learning more about Your word, Your plan for a father and daughter relationship, and Your design for authentic womanhood. We thank You for this precious time together and know that it is all possible only because of You. During our time together tonight, _____ (daughter's name) and I ask that You guide our conversation and help us bring all of our joy back to You and give You all the glory. We love You and want to know You more intimately each and every day.

In Jesus' name we pray,
Amen

3-2-1 Action! Activity

Dads, rather than thinking of tonight's season finale Episode as an ending, I encourage you to use tonight's Episode as a launch point for your father/daughter relationship. Yes, celebrate your accomplishments throughout the season. Yes, help teach her about the Proverbs 31 woman with the Orthodox Jewish translation. Yes, show her that chivalry is not dead and that men should treat her with respect and dignity.

But don't stop developing the relationship with your daughter. She needs you in her life. She looks to you for advice. She looks to you for support. She looks to you for affirmation. She looks to you in how to handle difficult situations. She looks at how you treat women. She looks at your work ethic. She looks at your prayer life. She not only needs you in her life, she desperately *wants* you in her life.

With this mindset, then, go eat some great food, enjoy the conversation, and create a memory that will last a lifetime.

The Dinner

Before you head out for dinner, make sure that you present the corsage to your daughter and offer to place it on her left wrist (unless she is left-handed, of course).

The dinner always starts with the drive. Make sure your vehicle is clean, inside and out. Open the car door at each stop. Open the door for her at the restaurant. Pull out her seat for her at the restaurant. Stand whenever she stands. Allow her to order first, even if the wait staff asks you first. Use proper table etiquette throughout your meal.

Dads, if this is not something you currently do on date nights with your wife or girlfriend, start now. Model to your daughter how a woman is supposed to be treated by a man.

The Conversation

Once you have both ordered your meal, take out your Bibles and ask your daughter the following questions:

1. Have you ever heard of the Proverbs 31 woman? If so, what have you heard?

2. Will you turn to Proverbs 31 and read verse 10 for me?

3. What does "virtuous" or "of noble character" or "good wife" mean to you? (depending on your daughter's version of the Bible). Why?

Next, explain how words can sometimes get lost in translation. For example:

- Burger King's "PooPoo Smoothie"—A mango-flavored bubble tea in China.

- "Barf Soap"—An Iranian detergent that means 'snow' in the Farsi language.

- The "Fart Bar"—In Poland, where this candy bar is made, the name translates to "lucky bar."

- "Pee Cola"—Bottled in Ghana—refreshing!

- Chevy Nova—Translated from English to Spanish literally means "No go."

Then, tell her you are going to read the translation of Proverbs 31:10 from the Jewish Orthodox Bible (Today's "SCRIPT"-ure):

> *A woman of valor who can find?*
>
> *Proverbs 31:10*

4. How would you define valor?

Next, share with her how Marilynn Chadwick explains how the woman of valor better depicts authentic womanhood as God intended—woman as both *nurturer* and *warrior*.

5. How does your impression of a virtuous woman differ from a woman of valor?

6. Explain.

7. Would you rather be described as a virtuous woman or a woman of valor? Why?

8. Who would you describe as a woman of valor? Would you be willing to tell me why?

Have your daughter take a pen and cross out virtuous or noble woman in her Bible and write woman of valor in its place. Then, have her highlight the passage.

Whether or not your appetizer or salad has arrived yet, go ahead and lead the conversation towards the Backstage Pass questions.

🎟 Backstage Pass

During your meal, take a few minutes to look back on all of the time that you spent together and then ask your daughter the following questions:

1. What has been your favorite Episode and why?

2. What was your least favorite Episode and why?

3. What was the most awkward or annoying Episode and why?

4. What Episode did you learn the most from and why?

5. If you could do a re-do of only one Episode, which one would you do and why?

6. What is one thing that you learned about me that surprised you during the season?

Don't forget to order dessert if you haven't already. Then, get ready for the Red Carpet Interview.

🎬 Red Carpet Interview

Red Carpet Questions for Dad

1. Let's start off with an easy question, Dad. What did you have for dinner tonight? How was it?

2. What do you see in me that shows that I am a woman of valor? How am I both nurturer and warrior?

3. Of all of the translation mishap examples, what is your favorite example?

4. What is your favorite memory of our entire season? Why?

Red Carpet Questions for Daughter

1. What did you order for dinner tonight and what restaurant did you pick?

2. When you hear the word "valor," what words or images immediately come to your mind?

3. Do you agree that women were meant to be both nurturer and warrior? Why?

4. Do you feel that you are more gifted as a nurturer, a warrior, or equally the same? Explain.

5. How many popcorn buckets would you give today's Episode? (Circle your choice)

Before you leave, ask the wait staff if they would be willing to take a picture of the two of you. Make sure to get the picture developed on photo paper and put it in a frame for your daughter within a week of the Season Finale Episode.

Hold the doors all the way to, and including, the car door. Thank your daughter for the lovely evening. Tell her how proud you are of her. Tell her how much you love her.

 Hannah's Take

I really want to become a woman of valor. I want to live the life that God intends for me to live because my plans never seem to work out quite right. I want to be perfect, but I think we all need to realize that only God is perfect.

We are all sinners, no matter what. We cannot be perfect in all that we do. God offered His forgiveness by sending His perfect son to die on the cross to save us all from our sins. We are washed clean of our sins through Jesus Christ, and if you have not accepted Jesus Christ as your savior, please read the ***Prayer to Accept Jesus Christ into Your Life*** at the end of this book to help you learn more.

As we pursue becoming a woman of valor, we cannot get stuck in all of the things we mess up because God offers forgiveness. Everything is part of His perfect plan that we simply cannot understand.

Just because God always forgives us *does not* give us a free pass to go on and just sin whenever we want just because we are forgiven. Then, we would not be pursuing becoming a woman of valor, now would we.

I really want you to remember that becoming a woman of valor is a process and to not get caught up in your mistakes. God has a perfect plan for us all, and there is no way that we can mess it up!

—Hannah

Post your father/daughter dinner photos on the *Friday Night Lights for Fathers Private Facebook Group.*

ACT III:
THE CEREMONY

CONGRATULATIONS!

Before we dive into ACT III, I want to personally congratulate both you and your daughter(s) on completing your *Friday Night Lights for Fathers and Daughters* 10-Episode season!

Now it's time to celebrate. Time to celebrate your father/daughter relationship. Time to reflect on all of the incredible memories you shared throughout the season and seal them with a ceremony that spotlights each of you.

If you read my first book, *Friday Night Lights for Fathers and Sons*, you know that I strongly believe in the power of ceremony to mark those special events in the lives of our children—to help them transition between child and young adult.

Here is an excerpt from my first book:

> Ceremonies are those special occasions that weave the fabric of human existence." Robert Lewis goes on to remind us to "Think back upon the significant moments in your life. With few exceptions, the value of those moments was sealed by ceremonies."[1]

Ceremonies truly seal the deal for those involved. Now that you have completed your 10-Episode season with your daughter, it's time to seal the deal. It's your opportunity to imprint the memories of your season not only with your daughter but with those whom you invite as well.

Dads, this will take some work, some planning, and a bit of time, but I can guarantee you that it will all be worth it.

Don't be overwhelmed. I will walk you through step-by-step from the planning all of the way through the presentation.

THE DAD'N'ME AWARD CEREMONY

Staying in line with the TV reality series theme, I thought it only natural to help you plan a celebrity-style award show. Although I can honestly say I have never watched an entire award show, I have seen clips and am familiar with the basic format.

Is it just me, or does it seem that there is a celebrity award show on TV at least once a week? From the Academy Awards to the Golden Globes and The Emmys to the Tony's, award shows are innumerable—and that's just for film. Now, add in music awards like MTV, BET, Grammys, AMA . . . and sports awards such as the ESPYs and the Heisman Trophy. The list goes on and on.

Our lives are inundated with award shows, but I can guarantee that anyone receiving one of the awards, whether it be an Oscar or a Grammy, each person will vividly remember the moment they received the award. For many, receiving this type of an award is a once in a lifetime opportunity, surrounded by family, friends, and fans.

I want to help you create this type of lasting memory for your daughter. Are you ready?

Overview

Why the Dad'n'Me Award? First of all, the Academy Awards are the most recognizable and most popular award show. Secondly, I really wanted the title to represent the two people that are celebrating the award. Therefore, using a bit of play on words, I titled the award the Dad'n'Me Award.

Before I go on, I know that some of you may be wondering why I didn't stay in line with the proper award for a television series, either the Golden Globes or the Emmys. Let me address that now—I didn't like either one. 'Nuf said.

The Dad'n'Me Award Ceremony will include the following sections:

- The Nominee Announcement
- Red Carpet Interview Video
- The Presentation of the Award Speech
- The Acceptance Speech
- The Afterparty

Dad, you will act as the emcee. Don't worry about making any jokes and please don't make any political wisecracks like many of the emcees seem to be doing nowadays. Keep this ceremony about your daughter only. Feel free to use the suggested script I have for you later in this section. You may also choose to customize your own unique script.

Dad's To-Do List (Before the Ceremony)

✓ Set and confirm date of the Dad'n'Me Award Ceremony (especially with your daughter!)
  - Plan on at least one month out to have time to complete the To-Do List.

- ✓ Create and Present a formal Dad'n'Me Award ticket/invitation to your daughter.
  - This can be handwritten, typed, or professionally made, depending on your time, ability, and budget. This ticket/invitation will start the anticipation and excitement for the award ceremony.

- ✓ Make a list of invitees
  - Immediate family, grandparents, pastor, close family friends, small group members, daughter's friends (and parents), and anyone else you and your daughter might want to invite.

  - This can be for the immediate family only or as many people as you like. Some of you are natural entertainers, and some of you might be, like me, more of a small group kind of entertainer.

- ✓ Send out invites/tickets (you decide)
  - Once the date is confirmed, send out invites/tickets via email, snail mail, eVite.com, Eventbrite.com, or via phone.

  - It's all right to include your daughter in this process; she may be more technically-versed when it comes to invites.

  - Make sure to have your invitees RSVP by a certain date so you can plan accordingly.

- ✓ Write a customized *Nominee Announcement*
  - You can use the sample script below if you would like.

  - Purchase an envelope for the announcement. A legal-sized #10 envelope will do. Feel free to decorate as you wish.

✓ Create the ***Red Carpet Interview Video***
  - Compile all of the Red Carpet Interview video clips you took throughout the season.

  - Don't let this overwhelm you. You have many options when it comes to video editing and compilation:

    - Do-it-yourself with

      - Microsoft Movie Maker

      - Apple iMovie

    - Ask a techy friend

    - Hire a freelancer at Fiverr.com or Upwork. com

  - Remember, this video has captured a slice of time with you and your daughter and deserves the time, effort, and perhaps a bit of money, to create it.

✓ Test video and audio equipment
  - Ensure that you have the correct equipment, adaptors, and other necessary items when showing your video live.

  - You may choose to download the clip as an .mp4 file or onto a DVD (or both).

✓ Prepare the ***Presentation of the Award Speech***
  - Write the presentation of the award speech

    - Explain why your daughter is receiving the award. I have a sample speech for you below.

  - Purchase The Dad'n'Me Awards

- The Dad'n'Me Awards are not stat-
  uettes like the Oscar or the Emmy,
  rather, they are "connection keychains" that will signify your season.

- I have designed the Dad'n'Me Award
  "connection keychain" for you and
  your daughter to wear.

- You can purchase two "connection
  keychains" (one for you, one for your
  daughter) at MarkLaMaster.com/
  shop

✓ Ask your daughter to prepare her *Acceptance Speech*
  - I have a sample Acceptance Speech below to
    guide her.

  - Don't help your daughter write this. Her
    Acceptance Speech will be much more powerful
    for you if you let her write this on her own or
    with the help of someone else.

✓ Plan for the *Afterparty*
  - The Afterparty is really just a fancy word
    that goes along with the theme of TV and
    Hollywood award celebrations.

  - I will provide you with a list of Afterparty ideas
    below.

Emcee Script (for Dad)
Emcee (Dad): Welcome to the Friday Night Lights for
Fathers and Daughters Dad'n'Me Award Ceremony.
  Tonight, we will be celebrating all the time that
_____ (your daughter's name) and I have

experienced over the past 10-Episodes of our first-ever TV season together.

From the Pilot Episode to the Season Finale, _____ (your daughter's name) and I have so much to celebrate.

And we want to celebrate all of it with you!

Thank you so much for coming tonight. Each of you is here for a reason, and each of you has made an impact in the life of _____ (your daughter's name). We want to celebrate you as well.

Nominee Announcement

Emcee (Dad): I would now like to introduce our Nominee for the Dad'N'Me Award:

Sample Script:

Our first and only nominee for the Dad'N'Me Award is _____ (daughter's name).

Clap Hands and wait for audience applause.

For the past 10-Episodes, I have had the honor and privilege of spending time with this lovely young woman: _____ (daughter's name).

Throughout our season together, _____ (daughter's name) and I have had a ton of fun together. We have had some deep conversations—some of which were pretty awkward. We had our share of bloopers and embarrassing moments. We laughed and cried, but most of all, we got to know each other better, and we both grew closer to God.

In just a few minutes, I will show you the Red Carpet Interview Video from our season together. But before I do, I want to share with you what _____ (daughter's name) and I talked about over the past 10-Episodes.

We started our conversation with a discussion on faith. We each chose our own One Word and talked about how we would pursue God in new ways. Next, we discussed body confidence and learned how God created us exactly the way He wanted us to be.

_____ (daughter's name) and I then moved on to how to pursue godly friendships and how to deal with our frenemies. Right after that, we set up social media guardrails and learned how social media influences our reputations.

Moving on, we discussed her dreams, goals, gifts, and talents. We put together a time capsule and look forward to God's plan for her future. In the following Episode, we discussed contentment and how to have a grateful attitude rather than having a sense of entitlement.

As we neared the last few Episodes, we went a bit deeper. We talked about boys and dating and God's plan for marriage. Next, we talked about sex—both God's plan and the science and statistics.

We then talked about the power of prayer, each creating our own prayer journals. Our season finale focused on Proverbs 31:10 and we discussed how God designed her to be a "woman of valor" and what that means in today's culture.

Let's give our nominee, _____ (daughter's name), a hand! (*Clap*)

Red Carpet Interview Video
Emcee (Dad): As with all award celebration shows, we, too, have a video to show you from our season together.

At the end of each Episode, _____ (daughter's name) and I asked each other Red Carpet Interview questions.

What you are about to see are clips of both of us answering those Red Carpet Interview questions.

Show video now.

Emcee (Dad): _____ (daughter's name) and I had so much fun filming these videos, and we hope you had just as much fun watching them.

And now, the moment you have all been waiting for.

And the winner is . . .

_____ (daughter's name)!

Begin clapping.

_____ (daughter's name), would you please stand next to me as I present you with the Dad'n'Me Award?

Once she is standing next to you, face your daughter and read her the Presentation of the Award script: (Here is a sample that you can build upon):

The Presentation of the Award Speech

Emcee (Dad): _____ (daughter's name), you are so beautiful—inside and out. I love you!

Tonight, I am proud to present you with this Dad'n'Me Award ("connection keychain")

Over the course of our 10-Episodes together, I want you to know how proud of you I am for all that you learned, for all that you shared with me, and for all that you taught me.

I love you so much, and I am so proud of the young woman you are becoming.

Are you all right if I share a few of my favorite memories with you?

Add a few highlights and memories from your season here.

I know that you have been through some struggles and some tough times as a young woman. And I know that you will experience more peaks and valleys throughout your life, but I am so encouraged by how strong of a person you are. Your faith is growing every day. You continue to make wise decisions about who you choose as friends. You continue to learn more about the gifts and blessings God has created in you. I am amazed at the maturity and discipline you have shown with social media and within the beauty and body-focused culture you live in.

_____ (daughter's name), I want you to know that I enjoyed each and every second of the time that we spent together. You are a fun person to be around, and I am so grateful for our relationship. I want you to know that I will always be here for you as long as I am able. Know that I am willing to talk to you about anything, anytime.

Tonight, _____ (daughter's name), I am presenting you with the Dad'n'Me Award. *(Hand your daughter her "connection keychain" now).*

During dinner at our final Episode, we talked a lot about Proverbs 31:10, which introduces a Woman of Valor.

_____ (daughter's name), you are this woman—this woman of valor. I want to mark this date, _____(today's date), as the day that you transitioned from my little girl to a young woman of valor.

My hope and prayer are that this "connection keychain" will serve as a constant reminder of who you are as a woman and who you are in God's kingdom.

On one side of the keychain, you will see, FNL4FD and a shield. The FNL4FD stands for our Friday Night Lights for Fathers and Daughters season together. The shield represents your strength as a woman, both a nurturer and a warrior.

On the back, you see Proverbs 31:10. May this always remind you that God is at the center of your life and that he designed everything about you. The Bible represents His Word and the cross represents His sacrifice for you and for me.

As you present the "connection keychain" *to your daughter*, say the following:

Emcee (Dad): _____ (daughter's name), I now present you with the Dad'n'Me Award.

Begin clapping.

To help commemorate our season together, I will always carry a memory of our season together with this matching "connection keychain." It will be a constant reminder of our time together and our growing father and daughter relationship.

Show your "connection keychain" now.

Congratulations! I love you and am so proud of the young woman you are becoming.

The Acceptance Speech

Dad, the next section is for your daughter only! Do not read.

Daughter: **Acceptance Speech** (Here is a sample for your daughter ONLY):

Dad, thank you so much for this award! I couldn't have done it without you. You have taught me so much over the past season.

Do you remember when . . . (*list out one of your favorite memories from the season here*).

I would have to say that the most annoying thing you did OR you asked me was . . . *(write out your memory here).*

My favorite Episode Activity was . . . *(describe your favorite Episode Activity and why here).*

But overall, my favorite memory from our season was . . . *(list out favorite memory here. This may be a specific moment or memory or a general memory, such as spending time with Dad.)*

I love you so much Dad and am so lucky to have you as a dad. Thank you so much for such a fun season and for all of the wonderful memories.

I would also like to thank . . . *(list out all of the people that have supported you over time—your mom, brother(s) and sister(s), grandparents, aunts/uncles, friends, pastor, teacher, coach, etc.)*

Finally, and most importantly, I would like to thank God for all that He has given me!

Thank you, again!

Emcee (Dad): Ladies and Gentlemen, let's give it up one more time for _____ (daughter's name)!

Emcee (Dad): That concludes our Award Ceremony. Now it's time for the Afterparty.

Before we begin the Afterparty, though, I just want to thank each and every one of you for your role in helping, encouraging, and leading _____ (daughter's name) into a godly young woman. We will be forever grateful to you.

Emcee (Dad): Now, let's have some more fun at the Afterparty.

The Afterparty

If I didn't know much about award celebrations, I know even less about the Afterparty. Fortunately, we have Pinterest and Etsy to help us out. After a bit of Afterparty research, I realized the most important item is food.

This made everything so much easier—why? Because I picked a few of Hannah's favorite foods and voilà, I knew what to have on the Afterparty menu.

Here are a few Afterparty ideas and some of Hannah's favorite snacks.:

- *Homemade Chocolate Chip Cookies*

    - Hannah and I would bake these from scratch from the time she was three or four years old.

- *Movie popcorn loaded with melted butter and peanut M&Ms*

    - This deliciously sweet and salty treat has become a LaMaster movie night tradition.

    - You don't have to go to a movie to pick up a tub of this buttery treat, stop by your local movie theater and get a tub or two!

- *Afterparty Candy Station*
  - Hannah loves candy. We filled multiple canning jars with several different kinds of Hannah's favorite candies and placed them on the table next to Hannah's other favorite snacks.

The Afterparty is a time for conversation, reminiscing, and connecting with the family and friends who have come to support your 10-Episode season and to acknowledge the young woman your daughter has become.

You can make the Afterparty as formal and fancy or as informal and simple as you like. Either way you choose, your daughter will always remember it.

Enjoy!

Please share any tips, questions, ideas, and memories from your Dad'n'Me Award Ceremony and Afterparty inside of the *Friday Night Lights for Fathers Private Facebook Group*. We can all help each other out to create the best experience for our daughters!

PRAYER TO ACCEPT JESUS CHRIST INTO YOUR LIFE

Below, are the most important 124 words in the entire book—period!

If you have been reading through this book and have been confused or have had questions about all of the Bible talk, the scripture, and the prayers, you are not alone. If you, while reading this book, have had a feeling you may never have experienced before, leading you to learn more about Jesus Christ—again, you are not alone. If you feel defeated or discouraged as a dad because of your past or current sins, mistakes, or thoughts, I encourage you to get down on your knees and read the 124 words below. It will literally change your life.

Jesus, I believe you are the Son of God, that you died on the cross to rescue me from sin and death and to restore me to the Father. I choose now to turn from my sins, my self-centeredness, and every part of my life that does not please you. I choose you. I give myself to you. I receive your forgiveness and ask you to take your rightful place in my life as my Savior and Lord. Come reign in my heart, fill me with your love and your life, and help me to become a person who is truly loving—a person like you. Restore me, Jesus. Live in me. Love through me. Thank you, God. In Jesus' name, I pray. Amen.[2]

Ransomed Heart Ministries
RansomedHeart.com

Perhaps you have already given your life to Jesus Christ, but feel led to share these words with your daughter. If this describes you and your daughter, I encourage you to share the prayer above with your daughter.

To be honest, if this is the only section of the entire book you read; and if, by reading this page, you, your daughter, or someone else you know, invites Jesus Christ into their life, writing this book was 100% worth it.

BEYOND FRIDAY NIGHT LIGHTS FOR FATHERS AND DAUGHTERS

My hope and prayer is that you and your daughter have developed a deeper and more meaningful relationship over the course of your season.

But don't stop now—keep the momentum going in your father-daughter relationship. Continue to schedule time in your calendar with your daughter. Continue to ask your daughter questions about her faith, her fears, and her future. Encourage her to pursue her dreams, develop godly friendships, and learn contentment in all that this life brings her way.

Most important of all though, be there for her. Listen to her. Help her develop into the woman of valor God designed her to be. Don't let this be your first and last season together. Get creative and design your own season in this Fathers and Daughters series. You can certainly modify any of the Episodes in this book or, better yet, work together and design your own. Check out the ideas other dads are sharing in the Friday Night Lights for Fathers Private Facebook Group. Sign up for my blog at MarkLaMaster.com, where I share faith-based fatherhood content on a consistent basis.

If you would like to take this whole fatherhood coaching to the next level, I would be honored to work with you individually, with your men's group, or speak at one of your upcoming events.

I will also be offering an online video course as a companion to Friday Night Lights for Fathers and Daughters, just as I have for Friday Night Lights for Fathers and Sons. You can check these courses out by going to dad-coaching. teachable.com

Lastly, my mission is to help dads develop deeper and more meaningful relationships with their kids and help them both grow closer to God. If this book has inspired you to get to know your daughter better and has helped bring you both closer to God, I would be honored if you would take five minutes or less to post an honest review on Amazon.com. Your reviews help other dads choose the best books and resources available to develop deeper and more meaningful relationships with their daughters in a faith-based format.

I am so grateful you purchased this book. May God bless your father and daughter relationship beyond your earthly expectations.

God Bless,

—Mark

ENDNOTES

Act I

Introduction
1. Westcott, Kevin. "73 Percent of Americans Binge Watch TV." Deloitte United States. March 22, 2017. https://www2.deloitte.com/us/en/pages/about-deloitte/articles/press-releases/deloitte-digital-democracy-survey-eleventh-edition.html.
2. Smith, Craig. "110 Amazing Netflix Statistics and Facts." DMR. August 07, 2017. Accessed June 15, 2017. http://expandedramblings.com/index.php/netflix_statistics-facts/.
3. Koblin, John. "Netflix Studied Your Binge-Watching Habit. That Didn't Take Long." The New York Times. June 08, 2016. Accessed June 16, 2017. https://www.nytimes.com/2016/06/09/business/media/netflix-studied-your-binge-watching-habit-it-didnt-take-long.html?_r=0.

A Dad's Particular Set of Skills
1. *Taken*. Directed by Pierre Morel. Performed by Liam Neeson. EuropaCorp, 2008. DVD.
2. Rossman, Sean. "Why Dads Matter, According to Science." USA Today. June 13, 2017. Accessed September 04, 2017. https://www.usatoday.com/story/news/nation-now/2017/06/13/why-dads-matter-according-science/377125001/.

3. Raeburn, Paul. *Do Fathers Matter?: What Science Is Telling Us about the Parent We've Overlooked*. New York: Scientific American/Farrar, Straus and Giroux, 2015.
4. Dobson, James. "11 Reasons Why Dads Matter to Daughters." Dr. James Dobson. Accessed September 04, 2017. http://drjamesdobson.org/blogs/dr-dobson-blog/dr-dobson-blog/2016/06/10/11-reasons-why-dads-matter-to-daughters.

Act II

Believe Episode

1. MacDonald, James. "It's the Whole Thing." *James MacDonald Bible Teaching*, 8 Mar. 2008, www.jamesmacdonald.com/teaching/devotionals/2008-03-03/. Accessed 17 Mar. 2017.
2. Ashcraft, Michael, and Rachel Olsen. "Change Your Life with Just One Word." *FaithGateway*, 28 Dec. 2014, www.faithgateway.com/change-your-life-with-just-one-word/#.WU1xumVJXpU. Accessed 23 June 2017.

S.I. vs S-I Episode

1. Ethridge, Shannon, and Stephen Arterburn. *Every Young Woman's Battle: Guarding Your Mind, Heart, and Body in a Sex-saturated World*. Colorado Springs, CO: WaterBrook Press, 2007. 58-59.
2. Amadei, Magalie, and Claire Mysko. "Definition of the Day: Body Confidence." 5 Resolutions to Transform the Fashion and Beauty Industries. October 12, 2009. Accessed April 2, 2017. http://5resolutions.blogspot.com/2009/10/definition-of-day-body-confidence.html.
3. Gresh, Dannah. *Raising Body-confident Daughters: 8 Conversations to Have with Your Tween*. Eugene, OR: Harvest House Publishers, 2015. 14.

4. Irwin, Stacey O'Neal. *Digital Media: Human-technology Connection.* Lanham: Lexington Books, 2016. 116.
5. Spector, Dina. "The Sports Illustrated Swimsuit Issue: A $1 Billion Empire." Business Insider. February 12, 2013. Accessed June 15, 2017. http://www.businessinsider.com/business-facts-about-the-sports-illustrated-swimsuit-issue-2013-2.
6. Hoyt, Jeff. "Billion-Dollar Bikinis." MoneyTips. February 17, 2016. Accessed April 14, 2017. https://www.moneytips.com/billion-dollar-bikinis.
7. Payne, Marissa. "Did Sports Illustrated's Swimsuit Issue Go Too Low with Hannah Davis's Bikini Bottom?" The Washington Post. February 05, 2015. Accessed April 16, 2017. https://www.washingtonpost.com/news/early-lead/wp/2015/02/05/did-sports-illustrateds-swimsuit-issue-go-too-low-with-hannah-daviss-bikini-bottom/?utm_term=.d9466df5d2a2.
8. Amos, Candace. "Hannah Davis Nearly Yanks Off Bikini Bottom for SI: Too Much?" Us Weekly. February 05, 2015. Accessed April 15, 2017. http://www.usmagazine.com/celebrity-style/news/hannah-davis-yanks-bikini-bottoms-sports-illustrated-swim-too-hot-201552.

Friends vs. Frenemies Episode

1. Simmons, Rachel. *Odd Girl Out: How to Help Your Daughter Navigate the World of Friendships, Bullying and Cliques - in the Classroom and Online.* London: Piatkus, 2012. 20-21.
2. Simmons, Rachel. *Odd Girl Speaks Out: Girls Write about Bullies, Cliques, Popularity, and Jealousy.* Orlando, FL: Harcourt, 2004.
3. Damour, Lisa. *Untangled: Guiding Teenage Girls through the Seven Transitions into Adulthood.* London: Atlantic Books, 2017. 58-59.

4. Keller, Timothy. *Friendships.* Gospel in Life. 2005. Accessed May 13, 2017. http://www.gospelinlife.com/friendship-9628

Waffles and Wi-Fi Episode
1. Sales, Nancy Jo. *American Girls: Social Media and the Secret Lives of Teenagers.* New York, United States: Vintage Books, 2017. 21.
2. Orenstein, Peggy. *Girls & Sex: Navigating the Complicated New Landscape.* New York, NY: Harper, an Imprint of HarperCollinsPublishers, 2017.
3. Weinberger, Jesse. *The Boogeyman Exists—and He's in Your Child's Back Pocket.* United States: CreateSpace, 2014.
4. Sass, Eric. "Girls lead on Snapchat, Instagram adoption." Mediapost. Accessed May 16, 2017. https://www.mediapost.com/publications/article/299271/girls-lead-on-snapchat-instagram-adoption.html?edition=102252
6. Abramovich, Giselle. "15 Mind-Blowing Stats About Generation Z." CMO.com by Adobe: Digital Marketing Insights, Expertise and Inspiration – for and by Marketing Leaders. June 12, 2015. Accessed May 13, 2017. http://www.cmo.com/features/articles/2015/6/11/15-mind-blowing-stats-about-generation-z.html#gs.30KHBR8.
7. Conner, Kate. *Enough: 10 Things We Should Be Telling Teenage Girls.* Nashville: B & H Publishing, 2014. 57-58.

Dream and Do Episode
1. Wild, Flint. "Katherine Johnson: A Lifetime of STEM." NASA. November 16, 2015. Accessed June 18, 2017. https://www.nasa.gov/audience/foreducators/a-lifetime-of-stem.html.
2. Bolden, Charles. "Katherine Johnson, the NASA Mathematician Who Advanced Human Rights with a Slide Rule and Pencil." Vanity Fair. August 22,

2016. Accessed June 20, 2017. http://www.vanityfair. com/culture/2016/08/katherine-johnson-the-nasa-mathematician-who-advanced-human-rights.

3. Shetterly, Margot Lee. *Hidden Figures: The American Dream and the Untold Story of the Black Women Mathematicians Who Helped Win the Space Race.* New York, NY: William Morrow, an Imprint of HarperCollins Publishers, 2016. 216-17.

4. Smith, Yvette. "Katherine Johnson: The Girl Who Loved to Count." NASA. November 20, 2015. Accessed February 12, 2017. https://www.nasa.gov/feature/katherine-johnson-the-girl-who-loved-to-count.

5. National Center for Fathering (NCF). "Ask your daughter questions." Accessed June 21, 2017. http://www.fathers.com/s7-hot-topics/daughters/ask-your-daughter-questions/.

"Grattitude" Episode

1. Singh, Rani. "The World's Richest Countries." Forbes. November 8, 2015. Accessed July 18, 2017. https://www.forbes.com/sites/ranisingh/2015/11/08/new-study-finds-a-better-way-to-measure-the-worlds-richest-countries/#6e69cc7f5075.

2. "25 Highest Income Earning Countries In The World." WorldAtlas. January 07, 2016. Accessed July 18, 2017. http://www.worldatlas.com/articles/the-highest-incomes-in-the-world.html.

3. Kauflin, Jeff. "The Countries With The Highest And Lowest Salary Expectations." Forbes. December 23, 2016. Accessed July 18, 2017. https://www.forbes.com/sites/jeffkauflin/2016/12/23/the-countries-with-the-highest-and-lowest-salary-expectations/#36dd0c682970.

4. Eyre, Linda, and Richard M. 4. Eyre. *The Entitlement Trap: How to Rescue Your Child with a New Family System*

of *Choosing, Earning, and Ownership*. New York: Avery, 2011. 114. Accessed July 18, 2017.

5. Welch, Kristen. *Raising Grateful Kids in an Entitled World: How One Family Learned That Saying No Can Lead to Life's Biggest Yes.* Carol Stream, IL: Tyndale House Pub, 2016.

6. Frank, Anne. *Anne Frank: The Diary of a Young Girl.* New York: Bantam Books, 1993.

7. U.S. Department of Commerce. *2015 Characteristics of New Housing.* Accessed July 18, 2017. https://www.census.gov/construction/chars/pdf/c25ann2015.pdf.

8. Andrews, Andy. *The Traveler's Gift Seven Decisions That Determine Personal Success, Local Print.* Thomas Nelson, 2010. 92-102.

A Sticky Situation Episode

1. Strasburger, V. "Adolescents, Sex, and the Media: Ooooo, Baby, Baby Q & A." *Adolescent Medicine Clinics* 16, no. 2 (2005): 269-88. Accessed August 15, 2017.

2. Committee on Communications. "Children, Adolescents, and Advertising." Pediatrics. December 01, 2006. Accessed August 15, 2017. http://pediatrics.aappublications.org/content/118/6/2563.

3. Gresh, Dannah. *What Are You Waiting For?: The One Thing No One Ever Tells You about Sex.* Colorado Springs, CO: Waterbrook Press, 2011. 116.

4. CDC. "Morbidity and Mortality Weekly Report (MMWR)." Centers for Disease Control and Prevention. June 21, 2017. Accessed July 16, 2017. https://www.cdc.gov/mmwr/volumes/65/ss/ss6506a1.htm.

5. Burns, Jim. *The Purity Code Conversations with Trusted Youth Experts on Healthy Sexuality.* United States?: Bethany House. 51.

6. CDC. "Adolescent and School Health." Centers for Disease Control and Prevention. August 04, 2017. Accessed

August 20, 2017. https://www.cdc.gov/healthyyouth/
sexualbehaviors/.

7. "11 Facts About Teens and STDs." DoSomething.org |
   Volunteer for Social Change. Accessed August 20, 2017.
   https://www.dosomething.org/facts/11-facts-about-
   teens-and-stds.

8. Sharpe, Jared. "UMass Amherst Sociologist Finds
   Abstinence 'Pledgers' Have Higher Risk of HPV,
   Non-Marital Pregnancies." Office of News & Media
   Relations | UMass Amherst. January 07, 2016. Accessed
   August 20, 2017. https://www.umass.edu/newsoffice/
   article/umass-amherst-sociologist-finds-abstinence.

9. NCSL. "Teen Pregnancy Affects Graduation Rates."
   National Conference of State Legislators. June 7,
   2013. Accessed August 21, 2017. http://www.ncsl.org/
   research/health/teen-pregnancy-affects-graduation-
   rates-postcard.aspx.

10. "Adverse Effects." Adverse Effects | Youth.gov. Accessed
    August 20, 2017. http://youth.gov/youth-topics/teen-
    pregnancy-prevention/adverse-effects-teen-pregnancy
    #_ftn.

11. Bush, Freda McKissic., Stan Guthrie, and Joe S. 11.
    McIlhaney. *Girls Uncovered: New Research on What
    America's Sexual Culture Does to Young Women*. Chicago,
    IL: Northfield Pub., 2011. 69.

12. McIlhaney, Joe S., and Freda McKissic. Bush. *Hooked:
    New Science on How Casual Sex Is Affecting Our Children*.
    Chicago: Northfield Pub., 2008.

13. Perry, Susan. "Neurotransmitters: How Brain Cells Use
    Chemicals To Communicate." Society for Neuroscience.
    May 16, 2011. Accessed August 20, 2017. http://www.
    brainfacts.org/brain-basics/cell-communication/
    articles/2011/neurotransmitters-how-brain-cells-use-
    chemicals-to-communicate/.

14. Vitaliano, Ed. "Bonded in The Brain: New Science Confirms View of Sex (10/2010)." Physicians for Life. December 1, 2010. Accessed August 31, 2017. http://www. physiciansforlife.org/bonded-in-the-brain-new-science-confirms-view-of-sex-102010/.

Weight or Wait Episode
1. Barr, Jeremy. "Teen Vogue Cuts Frequency to Four Issues a Year." Ad Age. November 07, 2016. Accessed May 12, 2017. http://adage.com/article/media/teen-vogue-cutting-back-issues-year/306647/.
2. "Seventeen Magazine." Seventeen | Hearst. 2017. Accessed May 12, 2017. https://www.hearst.com/magazines/seventeen.
3. "Fast Facts: Girls' Life Magazine." *Girls' Life.* Accessed May 12, 2017. http://www.girlslife.com/docs/2015GL_MktgFacts.pdf.
4. Jarmusch, Olivia. *When Life Feels Like a Taylor Swift Song: A Girl's Guide to Boys.* Crown of Beauty Magazine.
5. Feldhahn, Shaunti, and Lisa Ann. Rice. *For Young Women Only.* South Africa: Christian Art, 2008.
6. Eastham, Chad. *The Truth about Guys: One Guy Reveals What Every Girl Should Know.* Nashville, TN: Tommy Nelson, 2012.
7. Burns, Jim. *The Purity Code: God's Plan for Sex and Your Body.* Minneapolis, MN: Bethany House, 2008. Kindle.
8. Freitas, Donna. *Sex and the Soul: America's College Students Speak out about Hookups, Romance, and Religion on Campus.* New York: Oxford University Press, 2008.

Draw Near and Pray Episode
1. Canfield, Jack. *Chicken Soup for the Christian Soul.* Deerfield, FL: Health Communications, 1997.
2. Jarmusch, Olivia. "The GLOW Issue." Http://www.crownofbeautymagazine.com/. November 2016. Accessed

August 20, 2017. http://www.crownofbeautymagazine.com/TheGLOWIssue.html.

3. George, Elizabeth. *A Young Woman's Guide to Prayer: Talking with God about Everything.* Eugene, Or.: Harvest House Pub, 2012.

4. Ellis, Marian Jordan. "Becoming a Woman of Prayer." Redeemed Girl Ministries. March 3, 2016. Accessed August 20, 2017. http://www.redeemedgirl.org/becoming-a-woman-of-prayer.

5. Garibaldi, Molly. "Prayer Journals." Throne of Grace. April 28, 2013. Accessed August 20, 2017. http://www.throneofgrace.com/prayer-journals/

Season Finale Episode

1. Edwards. Haley. *11 Product Names That Mean Unfortunate Things in Other Languages.* Mental Floss. April 15, 2012. Accessed August 21, 2017.

2. Chadwick, Marilynn. *Woman of Valor: Discovering the courage and strength God gave you.* Harvest House Publishers. Kindle Edition. 2017.

Act III

1. LaMaster, Mark. *Friday Night Lights for Fathers and Sons: Schedule a 10-game winning season to help develop your son into the man God intended him to be.* Columbus, Ohio. United States: Author Academy Elite. 2015.

2. Ransomed Heart Ministries. *A Prayer to Receive Jesus Christ as Savior.* https://www.ransomedheart.com/prayer/prayer-receive-jesus-christ-savior. Accessed September 15, 2017.

CAST

_____ (Dad's name)
_____ (Daughter's name)

Credits

Executive Producer	God
Assistant Producer	Jen LaMaster, my bride of 20 years!
Assistant Director	Hannah LaMaster
Production Assistant	Lincoln LaMaster
Editor	Chris O'Byrne Founder, JETLAUNCH
Bravery Consultant	Jason W. Freeman
Stage Director locations	Multiple Caribou Coffee
Creative Director	Debbie O'Byrne, JETLAUNCH
Publisher	Author Academy Elite
Extras	Igniting Souls Tribe Members
	Friday Night Lights for Fathers and Daughters VIP Book Launch Team Members

WANT TO COMMEMORATE YOUR FRIDAY NIGHT LIGHTS FOR FATHERS AND DAUGHTERS 10-EPISODE SEASON?

Grab your Connection Keychains today!

The Connection Keychains can be presented during the Dad'n'Me Award Cermony to help seal your 10-Episode season together and serve as a constant reminder of your father/daughter relationship!

**Grab your Connection Keychains today:
MarkLaMaster.com/Shop**

BRING MARK INTO YOUR ORGANIZATION

Hi, I'm Mark.
Want me to speak at your next event?

I know the importance of selecting the right speaker for your next event. Hire a great speaker and your event is a hit. Hire the wrong speaker and you will get grief for a long time. If you are looking for an engaging, refreshing, and uplifting speaker for your next event, I want to help make your decision easier. I will customize each message to achieve your organization's needs and exceed your expectations.

Start the Conversation
MarkLaMaster.com/Speaker

"Mark is an engaging and dynamic speaker. He has a heart and passion for father/child relationships and sports. His speaking connects with both youth and adults. I would highly recommend Mark for your next event!"

—James Bolin, Area Director, Minnesota FCA

CPSIA information can be obtained
at www.ICGtesting.com
Printed in the USA
FFOW02n2242180418
46262126-47689FF